Reach for the Top

Reach for the Top

*A Woman's Guide to
Success in Business and Management*

Marilyn Davidson

PIATKUS

© 1985 Marilyn Davidson

First published in 1985 by Judy Piatkus (Publishers) Limited of London
Reprinted 1985

British Library Cataloguing in Publication Data

Davidson, Marilyn
   Reach for the Top
   1. Women executives
   I. Title
   658.4'2   HF5500.2
   ISBN 0-86188-497-3 Hbk
   ISBN 0-86188-300-4 Pbk

Typeset by Tradespools Ltd, Frome, Somerset.
Printed and bound by Butler and Tanner Ltd, Frome, Somerset.

Jacket/cover designed and illustrated by Ken Leeder

To the memory of my grandmothers – Florence Eyre
and Florence Robinson

Acknowledgements

I am most grateful to those people I interviewed and all those who gave their time and valuable advice. In particular, I would like to thank my sister Sue and my Aunt Jean (for her typing assistance), Barbara Douglas, Jean Watkins, Barbara Blyth, Colette Jarvis, Elizabeth MacDonald-Brown and Sheila Needham. Many thanks to Gill Cormode for her editing and helpful advice and suggestions. And a final special thankyou to Howard.

Contents

CHAPTER 1

Introduction

'If half your resources are women, a sensible country makes sure it doesn't waste them.'

Baroness Young, presenting the UMIST/American Express *'Women in Management'* Lecture, 1983

Despite the recession, unemployment and subtle political moves to keep women out of the workforce, more and more women are working than ever before. Over the last few years the number of women entering professional and managerial positions has increased considerably, and in several European countries more than 14% of managers and administrators are female. In Britain, the figure has reached 18%; in the United States it is an impressive 30%.

But there is still a serious shortage of women in management positions in Britain. If you feel that a managerial career is for you, *don't be put off* just because the majority of managers are male! It is up to the women managers of today and tomorrow to redress the balance. I hope that this book will act as an impetus for both women and employers to help change and improve the position of all women in management.

Different types of people make good managers. If you are contemplating a managerial or administrative career, or if you are already practising managerial skills, you will probably have one thing in common: you will enjoy dealing with people and policies. It has been estimated that between 70% and 90% of a manager's time is spent communicating – talking with people either on a one-to-one basis, such as on the telephone, or in a meeting or conference. Surprisingly, some women who are in professional and administrative positions tend to underestimate the managerial skills involved in their jobs. I remember a girlfriend of mine, who was about to be offered a partnership in the advertising agency in which she worked, commenting over lunch:

'You know, I've never considered myself a "woman manager", and I don't think I've ever read a management book in my life!'

When I asked her to describe to me just exactly what her job involved, she replied:

'Well, I have to manage budgets of several thousands of pounds, organise meetings, liaise continually with clients, supervise the people we sub-contract, and help manage the day-to-day running of the office.'

Then she laughed:

'I've used the word "manage" quite a bit, haven't I!'

Just because your job title may not include the description 'manager', 'administrator', or 'executive', it does not mean that you are not using skills associated with management and administration. Management is about individuals who are appointed by a company or organisation to control its day-to-day running, to plan and implement company policy, to achieve objectives relating to production and/or sales of goods or services, and to promote and develop strategies relating to product marketing. There are no real clear distinctions between the different levels of management. In every organisation there is a pyramid of managers, and while the majority of people who choose a career in management think in terms of senior and general managers, these in fact are the smallest sections and the bulk of managers remain on the middle rung of the managerial ladder.

Put in a nutshell, management is an activity aimed at making the best use of available resources in order to achieve a given objective. Therefore, as a woman, whether you are a television producer, a school's head of department, a buyer, a supervisor, or someone's secretary/personal assistant, you will most certainly be involved in management activities and *this book is for you.* I have used the word *manager* in the broadest possible sense and it is applicable to *all* women whose work requires them to incorporate a managerial role of some kind.

Even if you are at home looking after children, in your role of 'household executive' you will be acquiring important business skills such as co-operation, planning, budgeting, contracting, organising and supervising (e.g. plumbers, electricians, mechanics, solicitors, baby minders, house purchasers, etc). All of these are valuable assets transferable to the world of business. There is no such thing as being 'just a housewife' – you could be a potential manager of tomorrow. Take heart from the experiences of a woman television researcher who told me how stressing these acquired skills had helped her return to work after a four-year break:

> 'I'm now a single parent and I needed to get back to work for financial reasons as well as for my own personal fulfilment. I know for a fact that a couple of hundred people applied for the researcher's job, and being a woman who hadn't worked in television before and had been at home for years, I thought my chances were nil. Then I thought, blow it. I'm not undermining my time at home – it was hard work and involved massive organisation, management, budgeting and personnel-type work. So I mentioned all of this during the interview and it must have worked. I got the job!'

This book aims to be a positive and constructive self-help source of reference directed at both women contemplating a career in management, business or administration (e.g. students, secretaries, mothers returning to work) and women who are already working in this field. Over the past few years I have interviewed and questionnaire-surveyed hundreds of women in all types of professional, managerial and administrative jobs as part of my research and consultancy work, and personal accounts from them about the situations they encountered and the coping strategies which worked best for them appear in this book. In addition, I shall draw on positive advice accumulated from numerous sources, including personal interviews with experts in the field (e.g. researchers, management trainers, career counsellors) and specific documented recommendations and exercises (e.g. proposals by authors, unions, and professional bodies). Each chapter will be summarised by listing recommended strategies and suggestions.

However, before going into more depth about how you should go about becoming a woman manager and how to overcome the problems that may lie in your path to the top, let's first put the position of women at work in perspective and look at the present situation in both Britain and Europe.

The position of women at work

Although the situation of women at work could be improved enormously, it's not all doom and gloom and many women are making headway in their chosen managerial and professional careers. But having said that, I am often amazed at the ignorance of some personnel officers and managers regarding the issue of working women. There is still a prevailing opinion among many that, with the economic recession and unemployment, this is not the time to be promoting women's opportunities. My response is that, economically, organisations can no longer afford *not* to utilise the talents of their female workforce to the full because, like it or not, women in this country generally work, and many aspire to leadership and management positions.

Some interesting official statistics were recently compiled by the UK Equal Opportunities Commission (EOC) in the form of a small reference card entitled *The Fact About Women Is . . .* For example, between the ages of 20 and 59 most women are in continuous employment, with an average break of only seven years while they are raising a family. (This break tends to be shorter for professional women.) This appears to contradict the attitude that money and effort spent on training women is lost when they marry and have children. More than half of all mothers with children under 16 go out to work (full or part-time), and almost two-thirds of all married women (64%) are either employed or looking for work.

I recall relating these facts to a senior male manager working in the oil industry in Scotland. He was so astounded that he told a colleague the next day that he'd had trouble sleeping and wanted to see the statistics in print himself! His wife had never worked and neither did any of his colleagues' wives and he assumed that this was the norm. In fact, although advertising agencies (particularly when promoting products such as washing powder and the like) would have us believe otherwise, only 5% of all households are made up of a working husband, an economically inactive wife and two dependent children.

Nevertheless, in spite of the introduction of equal pay legislation by European countries, differences in pay between men and women persist, due partly to the fact that working women are concentrated in the lower echelon jobs. When I examined the average earnings of men and women in the textile industry, the food, drink and tobacco industry, electrical engineering, and the chemical industry in six countries – Germany, France, Italy, the Netherlands, Belgium and the UK – I found that women's average earnings (for 1980) were below average national earnings. The greatest gap between men's earnings and women's earnings is in Germany, then the UK and the Netherlands, and the narrowest in Italy and France. In the UK, for example, women's pay has dropped from around 75% of men's in 1977 to 73.9% in 1982. (Hopefully, the Equal Pay for Work of Equal Value Amendments of 1984 should give it another boost, even though it is still fraught with loopholes.)

Throughout all the European countries there is still job segregation based on gender – the arbitrary division between 'men's jobs' and 'women's jobs', which is so often taken for granted. In all the EEC countries over 50% of women are employed in the services sector, which includes retail, trade, education, health care and clerical duties. Approximately 20–25% of women workers are employed in the textile and food industries, and a large number in the chemical and electronics industries. Women's advance into what have been traditionally men's jobs is still very small. In the UK, for instance, the Economic Activity Tables of the 1981 Census, published in 1984, illustrate that in the seven occupation orders where women were outnumbered by men by more than 10 to 1 – professional and related in science, engineering and technology; managerial; security and protective services, processing, metals and electrical; construction and mining; transport and storage; miscellaneous – these accounted for only 19% of the entire female workforce *both in 1971 and 1981*. No inroads had been made.

The position of women as managers

On a more optimistic note, there is growth in the proportion of women now *entering* many of the formerly male-dominated jobs, including the field of management. Table 1.1 shows comparative figures for the United States and a selection of European countries. In the States, with the strongest legislation affecting the employment of women, 30·5% of managers and administrators are women, followed by the UK with 18·8%.

Table 1.1 *Women as a percentage of administrative and managerial workers in selected countries*

Country	Year	Salaried and wage earning workers
United States	1980	30·5
United Kingdom	1979	18·8
German Fed. Rep.	1978	16·7
France	1975	16·3
Norway	1978	14·2
Sweden	1975	11·2
Eire	1972	4·9
Spain	1978	2·4

Sources: ILO Yearbook of Labour Statistics, Geneva, 1979; EEC Labour Force Survey, 1979; US Census Bureau, 1980

Note: The occupational classifications are not identical for every country

In America there have been tremendous strides in the past decade, according to a recent census report. Between 1970 and 1980 the proportion of US women in traditionally male-

Table 1.2 *Female membership of selected professional Institutes and Associations, 1980*

Professional Institute or Association	% Women
Hotel Catering/Institutional Management	44·8
Institute of Personnel Management	30·0
British Medical Association	21·5
Institute of Health Service Administration	14·3
Institute of Bankers	13·0
The Law Society	11·8
The Chartered Insurance Institute	9·7
The Royal Town Planning Institute	7·1
The Rating and Valuation Association	5·9
Association of Certified Accountants	5·0
Institute of Chartered Accountants	4·2
Institute of Marketing	2·4
Institute of Chemical Engineers	1·7
British Institute of Management	1·5
Royal Institution of Chartered Surveyors	1·1
Institution of Works Managers	0·9
Institute of Building	0·4
Institute of Mechanical Engineers	0·3
Institution of Production Engineers	0·2

Source: Rosalind Miles, *Danger: Men at Work*, 1983, p. 27

dominated executive, managerial and administrative occupations rose from 18·5% to 30·5%. The proportion of public administrators and officials who are women rose during the decade from 21·7% to 33·6%; women financial managers from 19·4% to 31·4%; and those in the field of personnel and labour relations from 21% in 1970 to 36% in 1980. It will be interesting to see how the corresponding UK figures develop over the next 10 years.

However, the occupations in which European women are most likely to be managers are still the traditionally female occupations, such as retailing, catering and personnel. They are also usually employed in the lower levels of management. In the UK this can be clearly illustrated by looking at the percentage of female membership of selected professional Institutes and Associations outlined in Table 1.2 and at Table

Table 1.3 *Women managers as a percentage of all managers in selected occupational groups UK, 1979*

Managerial group	% Managers who are women
General management	3·3*
Managerial	
Production, works and maintenance	20·3
Managers and works foremen	4·6
Site and other managers (building and civil engineering)	2·9
Transport managers	3·4
Managers in warehousing and materials handling	2·7
Office managers	19·1
Managers in wholesale and retail distribution	30·4
Publicans, restauranteurs and club stewards	41·6
All managers, but excluding those in office, wholesale and retail distribution, publicans, restauranteurs and club stewards	10·1

Source: EEC Labour Force Survey, 1979
* 1981 figures

1.3 which shows women managers as a percentage of all managers in certain occupational groups.

Even so, there is a noticeable trend in some European countries for more women graduates to enter industry. In the UK, more than 40% of students currently studying for management or business degrees are women, and they make up over 10% of the total Master of Business Administration (MBA) students. But, while it appears easy for women to gain employment at the lower levels of an organisation, it is still proving very difficult for them to reach upper middle and senior management positions. In the UK in 1981, of the 18·8% of female managers and administrators, only 3·3% of general management jobs were held by women.

The major reasons for the absence of women in management are complex and numerous and include women's attitudes and behaviour, lack of opportunity, and prejudice. If the results from studies investigating manipulation of sexual behaviour from an early age are anything to go by, it's not surprising that females steer away from male-dominated occupations and leadership positions. According to Dr John Nicholson of Sussex University, this is easily proved. Take an infant of either sex and dress it in either a pink or blue bonnet, then take a random sample of 20 adults and study their reactions. In its blue bonnet the child is a mischievous, energetic little sod who is given a 'manly' hammer to play with; in pink, it's a flirtatious hussy and given a soft toy. Ask most people to describe male and female characteristics and men are immediately said to be assertive, strong, logical, leaders, scientific, unemotional and aggressive. Women, on the other hand, are described as passive, weak, anxious, caring, timid and so on. With this kind of stereotyping from a very early age, attitudes and motivations are undoubtedly moulded and are often difficult to change.

At one time or another we have all been guilty of mistaking the female voice on the other end of the phone as being that of the secretary rather than the boss, or the woman in the hospital waiting room in the white coat as a nursing assistant rather than the surgeon. I once interviewed a male general manager who for the previous hour had gone to great lengths to tell me how much he wanted to employ and encourage women to go into engineering. As a final question I asked him what he thought made a good engineer:

> 'Well, *he* has to be strong, *he* has to be highly mobile and *he* doesn't have to mind mucking in sometimes and getting *his* hands dirty!'

There is no doubt that women have fewer opportunities to enter professional and managerial positions compared to men, and this is due mainly to their limited educational and vocational training. Throughout all the European countries there is still a marked stereotyped division between the courses taken by males and females within both academic and vocational subjects. On the whole, girls still opt for shorter courses, often in welfare and domestic subjects, leading to lower marketable skills and qualifications compared to their male counterparts. The 1976 Eurostat Statistics showed that women, as a proportion of all students in higher education in all the EEC countries, were seriously under-represented. In 1976, the lowest proportion of women students was in the Netherlands at only 30·5% and the highest percentage of 46·4% was in France. These compared to 41·5% in the UK. Women in all the EEC countries going into higher education still tend to be concentrated in subject areas such as psychology, education, languages and sociology. A very small percentage of females take science subjects, usually either chemistry or biology. Males, on the other hand, dominate subjects such as physics, mathematics, technology, philosophy and economic sciences. These curricula constraints have been acknowledged by the European Commission. The split in the school curriculum between males and females occurs with domestic and craft studies at the beginning of secondary schooling, and with technical and science subjects from about the age of 14. This division is also enhanced by the widespread use of sex-role stereotyping in teaching materials, along with teachers' attitudes.

When I was at school, both my maths and chemistry teachers (who were both men) made it clear that boys were naturally good at maths and science, whereas it was a great exception for a girl to do well in these subjects. I once came second in a chemistry exam and my teacher was so astounded that he had to recheck my examination paper. And according to my Latin teacher, as a girl I'd never be any good at Latin, but I wasn't to worry as it wasn't my fault – it was all to do with my smaller brain! Similar attitudes still prevail today and recent studies show that, regardless of whether teachers are male or female, when facing a mixed class of boys and girls they will encourage verbally and non-verbally the boys to participate more than the girls, and also spend more time communicating with the boys. Indeed, it's mainly in single sex schools where, devoid of male competition, girls are more likely to study technical and science subjects. All in all, with far fewer women than men having experienced a vocationally-oriented basic education, it is not surprising that fewer women employees participate in technical and industrial training.

Nevertheless, the Labour Force Survey for 1979 indicated that there had been a marginal increase in women's share of management jobs, especially in non-traditional areas of work for women. But due to indirect and direct discrimination and prejudice from employers, personnel procedures, organisational policies and climate, as well as personal attitudes, women managers (potential and actual) face additional barriers compared to men. If they hope to succeed in their chosen field, women are expected to follow the typical male career patterns which involve high mobility and continuous work histories. Also the influence of family life on women's careers is still far greater than it is on men's, and in order for both men and women to reconcile their employment and family responsibilities improvements are required in maternity and paternity rights, re-entry schemes (including part-time work and job sharing) for women wishing to return to their jobs after having children, child-care facilities and more flexible working arrangements.

The other major burden experienced by married working women (especially those with children) is the lack of domestic help and support given by husbands and partners. Consequently, taking on the role of chief homemaker *and* having a full-time job increases a woman's workload enormously. This is still the case even in the more 'liberated' US and a very recent study there found that the working wife spends an average of 26 hours per week on housework while her husband spends 26 minutes! A three-year study of 1,400 dual career families with children under the age of 11 showed that only one American father in five helped with childcare. The situation is quite similar in Europe: in Denmark a survey by the Ministry of Labour discovered that the working wife spends an average of 21 hours per week on housework compared to the one hour 45 minutes spent by her husband. An even more astounding result emerged from a Dutch survey which illustrated that the wife working outside the home received an average 8·9 hours help from her husband a week, compared to 9·7 hours of domestic help a week from the husbands of *full-time* housewives! Interestingly, of the 60 women managers interviewed in our book *High Pressure*, almost every one maintained that when it came to the crunch *they* did more home duties than their partners.

Not only do attitudes vary somewhat from country to country towards working women but also from region to region. In Britain the highest percentage of women managers (as a percentage of total managers) are located in the South East including Greater London (28·8%), with the lowest percentage (2·6%) found in Northern Ireland, closely followed by East Anglia (3·8%) and the North (5·5%). My own research tends to confirm that the further north and/or the more rural, the greater the likelihood of encountering prejudice and discrimination towards working women. It seems that Manchester is therefore a far more suitable location for the Equal Opportunities Commission (EOC) than London! In the words of a female personnel officer in Scotland:

'People in England have little idea how *un*liberated most Scottish people are in relation to equal opportunities for women at work – especially concerning management positions. There is still this ingrained belief in most Scotsmen that a woman's place is most definitely in the home and if she works, it's for pin money. In my district, one company was considering introducing paternity leave and the local newspaper got hold of it and plastered it all over their front page in a patronising manner, namely: "Are we Scots going soft in the head!" Needless to say, the company involved dropped the scheme. Interestingly, during the suffragette movement, Scottish women were some of the most militant.'

CHAPTER 2

Choosing Your Career in Management

'Women managers should stop pretending to be surrogate men. Instead, they should look at themselves and their own needs and then work out what they want from their careers.'

Judi Marshall, *Women Managers: Travellers in A Male World*, 1984

Choosing the field of management that's right for you

Whatever your situation regarding your work life at the moment, it's important to think carefully about the field of management you would like to pursue. The aim of this chapter is to help you prepare, choose and plan your career – something that women tend to do to a lesser extent than men. Let's first outline what sort of jobs offer 'management' careers.

What are the jobs?

As mentioned in Chapter 1, management covers a vast range of jobs and anyone who controls the work of other people 'manages'. If you think you want to go into management in business, the careers to choose from include:

Production e.g. Manager of an engineering section
Purchasing and supply e.g. Buyer for a department store chain

Business functions e.g. Accountant or Finance Officer
Personnel e.g. Personnel Officer
Marketing/Advertising e.g. Film Producer in an advertising
   agency
Shipbroking and freight forwarding e.g. Antiques Shipping
   and Packaging Specialist
Arts administration e.g. Theatre Administrator, Art Gallery
   Director
Housing management e.g. Estate Agents Manager
Recreational management e.g. Manager of a sports complex

Or there are management services, which include:

Operational research e.g. Occupational Psychologist
Computing e.g. Computer Resources Manager in the Health
   Service
Work study, organisation and methods e.g. Management
   Consultant
Management training e.g. Management Training Officer

   These lists are by no means exhaustive and there are plenty
of other occupations which offer management opportunities,
such as education, medicine, etc.

Using career services

You should always make full use of careers guidance and
advisory services when choosing (and changing) your career
path. All education authorities are compelled to provide a
careers service, and all adults can obtain free career advice
from their local Careers Service Office (listed in your local
telephone directory under 'Careers'). The Manpower Services
Commission (MSC) offers numerous free services including
the Professional and Executive Recruitment Consultancy
Service (PER), and a Careers and Occupational Information
Centre (COIC) based at the MSC Headquarters in Sheffield.
The MSC Training Division also organises the TOPS courses
(Training Opportunities Schemes) offering a wide variety of
technical, commercial and production skills training, details of

which are obtainable from your local Careers Office, Job Centre or Employment Office.

Your local education authority (LEA) awards grants for many courses and you will need to apply to the LEA for an application form. There are also a number of bodies which are potential sources of small grants, such as the British Federation of University Women. A number of professional Institutes and Industry Training Boards give financial aid/scholarships for training/study (e.g. the Food, Drink and Tobacco Industry Training Board) and it is worth approaching any appropriate bodies with which you or your employer have an association.

Finally, important resource and career advice can be obtained by joining two associations which were formed specifically to offer support for women in management – Women in Management and the National Organisation for Women's Management Education (NOWME). The Women in Management association offers very useful fact sheets to members, including *Sources of Information on Careers Guidance and Advisory Services*; *Sources of Training Assistance, Grants and Loans*, and *Companies and Agencies Specialising in the Employment of Women*. NOWME was established in order to promote positive action in the area of women's management education and to encourage links between women managers via newsletters, conferences and a members' directory.

Female- versus male-dominated management fields – the pros and cons

Undoubtedly, it is easier for you as a woman to enter traditional female management positions in areas such as catering, retail and personnel. However, this only helps to perpetuate the division between 'male' and 'female' management jobs – the latter usually being of lower status and offering lower salary ceilings. In other words, if you enter these fields ensure that the choice is yours and not someone else's 'persuasive guidance'.

Jane is a 28-year-old Personnel Officer and she describes the advantages and disadvantages of working in Personnel:

'I didn't have a degree but joined my company as a

23

management trainee after leaving school with 'A' levels. To be honest with you, I was very good at the buying side of the business while I was being trained, but in this company all the buyers are male. Consequently, I was persuaded to go into Personnel – yet another of the female "caring" professions. I wish I'd known then what I know now. Personnel tends to have limited promotional prospects unless you're in a large organisation, and when it comes to senior personnel positions – men dominate. I do have female colleagues though, therefore I don't suffer from feelings of isolation or performance pressure by being a test case for future women; both of which I would have had to endure if I'd become the first woman buyer. Nevertheless, if I'd stuck to my guns and insisted on becoming a buyer, I would be in middle/senior management by now.'

The low percentage of female membership of selected Professional Institutes and Associations in 1980 gives some indication of the degree of male dominance (see Table 1.2). Clearly, the world of engineering has the least women and it seems appropriate that the Equal Opportunities Commission should have made 1984 the 'Women into Science and Engineering Year' (WISE). It is important that women are encouraged to enter the (previously) male preserves such as engineering, and many women thrive on the challenge of breaking into new territory. But as a woman you need to be aware of the coping strategies required to deal with the pressures of being a 'pioneer woman', including the acquisition of support systems.

Joan is a 32-year-old and one of the first female engineers to be employed by one of the largest industrial concerns in the UK:

'I chose the field of engineering mainly because it wasn't a typical female career and was therefore much more of a challenge. However, I think women should prepare themselves when entering male domains and accept that there is going to be this pressure on you to prove yourself as you're a woman breaking ground for future women. You have got to get used to fighting for things such as working on sites, etc.

24

You have to learn how to cope with men who have never worked with or for women before. To a certain extent, you have to be better than your male colleagues and you most definitely have to learn to sell yourself. Often women have problems in that area and confidence and assertion courses, as well as support from network groups such as other female engineers, are essential.

'There are no female managers in engineering in this company and I am determined to be the first. I'm at a disadvantage having no female managers to look to as role models, but I have a very supportive boss and I'm going to make it!'

A woman should not only be wary of being channelled into traditional female management areas, but also of accepting 'token' management positions which in reality have limited salary prospects, authority or career advancement possibilities. Today, women managers in Britain still earn less than men managers. A survey of women graduates from the Manchester Business School carried out in 1981, found that the women's salaries after graduation were, on average, only 94% of the men's. While part of the problem stems from the kind of low-paying fields of management which women have entered (e.g. food, retail trade and general office administration), the problem also comes from women managers themselves who, like the majority of working women, are far less concerned about pay levels then men. In a study I carried out with Cary Cooper for the MSC we surveyed 696 female managers and 185 male managers in all sorts of industries, management fields, and levels, and even though women managers at all levels of the managerial hierarchy were earning less than their male counterparts, it was the men who complained about dissatisfaction with their pay, not the women! (See the MSC publication *Women Managers: Their Problems and What can be done To Help Them.*) Salary level is often equated with seniority and power, and if women want to establish themselves in management careers in senior positions they have got to start by no longer accepting inferior salary scales to men.

Getting qualified

The graduate and the non-graduate

In such a competitive job market as management it would be unrealistic not to acknowledge the importance of educational attainment and qualifications. Unfortunately, as described in Chapter 1, females are given a less useful, less marketable, education at school and University in the arts subjects compared to males who are steered into the more marketable and practical maths and science subjects. In the 25–34 age group, only 2½% of women as opposed to 7½% of men have University degrees or equivalent qualifications; 59% of women as opposed to 48% of men have no formal qualifications of any kind.

Whilst there are no laid-down rules concerning the entry qualifications for management, in practice a degree or professional qualification is usually a prerequisite for senior management, and four 'O' levels for middle management. Naturally, there are men and some women who have become 'senior' executives with few or no qualifications, but they are the exceptions rather than the rule.

The UK University Statistical Record shows that from the early to late 1970s, there was a 33% increase in women graduates entering industrial employment; the number of women in finance and accounting rose from 14% to 23% in that period; in legal work from 25% to 32%, in personnel management from 51% to 62%; and in marketing, selling and buying from 28% to 36%. This trend has been reinforced by the increasing number of women taking University courses in management. (In 1984 over 40% of the total management students in the largest University management departments were female, compared to only 10% in 1973.) Interestingly, women tend to gain the better class of degrees in management sciences and entering the lower rungs of management is often not a problem, it is trying to get past the upper middle to senior management hurdles where the barriers begin to come down. One young female management graduate commented:

> 'They've only recruited professional women in our department in the past few years. Consequently, most of us are

young and in junior management positions. We are tolerated and for many of the men we are something of a novelty. I think the problems will begin when we start to fight for higher management positions.'

If you are thinking of taking a University course in management or related subjects, write to the relevant Universities, Polytechnics and Business Schools for prospectuses, and consult the CRAC Course Guides, CNAA Directory of First Degree and Dip.HE Courses, and *Which Degree*. The Open University is also offering an Educational Advisory Service Project for adults. If at all possible, try and visit the University department which offers a course of interest, either privately or by taking advantage of 'open days'. The personal approach is always best. I know of numerous women who have gained places at Universities (especially at post-graduate level) by ringing up the Head of Department and making an appointment to go and see him or her. It shows initiative, determination and eagerness; and, as in the business world, it's often not *what* you know, but *who* you know.

It's never too late

If you have no qualifications, then do not despair. It is never too late. Remember, educational institutions usually welcome mature students with open arms – they are more reliable, highly motivated and conscientious as students and often get good results. *The Guardian* recently reported the case of a Mrs Hesketh, who was one of the speakers at a 'Second Chances for Women' course being run by The Industrial Society:

'Sheila Hesketh began her working life in a clerical position. After producing two children she became a part-time waitress at North West Gas, then a full-time clerical officer. She took five 'O' levels and an 'A' level in economics in her mid-thirties, before studying for the Institute of Personnel Management exams. She was promoted to trainer at North West Gas, where she is now a manager. "It's been fascinating," sums up the 49-year-old grandmother, who next plans to take an Open University degree.'

And so, if you feel you lack qualifications, it's worth following the useful suggestions made by Jenny Glew in her book *Women at Work*.

1. Get your basics like 'O' levels.

2. Try for a Business Education Council General Diploma Course which can open up a whole host of opportunities for further study or work in the business world. General award courses are often available on a day release basis as part of a job.

On the other hand, if you have a few 'O' levels Jenny Glew suggests you could:

1. Go on to do an 'A' level course – full- or part-time (make sure you choose the right subjects).

2. Try to get on a course leading to a BEC National Diploma in business studies as an alternative. It's accepted by many professional bodies as an entrance qualification for those wanting a career in banking, insurance, administration, management, the Civil Service, etc. (Contact the Department of Education and Science for a leaflet on Diploma in Management Studies.)

3. Take other diploma courses to qualify you for a particular field, such as catering, art and design, engineering, etc.

4. Once you've got 'A' levels or a diploma, you've got a much bigger choice of going on to further study, such as a Higher National Diploma or a degree full- or part-time. Don't forget, there is always the Open University, and there are four-year sandwich degrees in Business Studies which include practical experience in commerce or industry. Most courses specialise in a particular branch or management function, e.g. finance, industrial relations, organisational behaviour, etc. As a mature candidate, you may be accepted with experience in lieu of qualifications so *don't be afraid of applying just because you don't have the relevant 'A' levels.*

Post-graduate training and qualifications include post-relevant professional qualifications and post BEC (Business Education Council) Higher National awards. Post-graduate courses tend to be either courses leading to specialist qualifications such as MSc., MBA, MPhil., Ph.D or are general management courses (these courses are also available at Business Schools). In addition, the CNAA Diploma in Management Studies is the largest management training scheme offered by around 90 Polytechnics and colleges. This scheme is particularly useful for women returning to work after a break. Finally, some Business Studies degrees also specialise in small business management, for those wishing to start their own company (another path for women to break into management, to be discussed in more detail in Chapter 3).

Beware, however, that in graduate recruitment a company may specify the need for particular subject degrees which may or may not help in the job. In these cases, once again the personal approach is often the answer, and I've known women who have turned up at the Personnel Officer's door in order to get a fair hearing. Employers often discriminate against women by advertising that 'the successful candidate will be between 25 and 35', the age range when many women are child-rearing and away from full-time employment. Again, don't be put off from applying. If possible do *not* state your age on the application form but rather put your date of birth. In a well-known test case under the Sex Discrimination Act, a civil servant named Belinda Price established that it was unlawful indirect discrimination against women to have an age bar of 28 for entry to the executive officer grade of the Civil Service. Late in 1979, as a direct result of this action, the Civil Service revised the age limit to 45.

So, if you are contemplating a career in management of any sort, certainly the best advice I can give is to get as well qualified as possible. Nevertheless, lack of qualifications, especially at degree level, puts many women at a disadvantage and sometimes hampers initiative and ambition. *Don't let it.* There are still women who have broken into senior management positions as non-graduates – and *you* could be one of them.

Career planning exercises

Having considered which type of management career attracts you and the qualifications you will need, the next essential step is to *plan your career*. This should be done sooner rather than later.

Men generally embark on career planning tactics earlier than women. Hennig and Jardim, in their book *The Managerial Woman*, isolated three patterns linked to the different concept that women have of a career:

1. The late career decision, defined as a conscious commitment to advancement over the long term and usually made some 10 years into their career, having concentrated primarily on the day-to-day aspects of their job during that period.

2. The passivity phase, where women claim that career advancement 'just happened, somebody did it for me'.

3. A pattern where there is emphasis on individual self-improvement as the critical factor in determining career development ... which in itself is related to passivity.

Therefore, many female managers, according to Hennig and Jardim, believe that a large number of women just drift into senior positions without clearly planning their career strategies. Consequently, it was not surprising to discover that of the 60 women managers interviewed in the pilot study I carried out with Cary Cooper and described in our book *High Pressure: Working Lives of Women Managers*, 50% of all women managers at all levels in the hierarchy had never set themselves a career life plan. Moreover, only 25% *had* set themselves a career life plan, and 25% only set themselves a career plan as their career developed. However, an interesting finding was that a larger percentage of the new generation of female managers appear to be planning their career paths compared to their predecessors. 43% of middle and 27% of junior managers were planning their career paths compared to only 13% of the current generation of senior female managers.

Nevertheless, women are less likely than men to be

identified for development and often receive less encouragement to manage their careers in the crucial early stages. Women managers generally have more work/life choices to make than men managers, and therefore you need to be more adaptable and innovative if you are to pursue your career aims. The following exercises will enable you to determine your long- and short-term career and personal plans.

Exercises: Long-term and Short-term Career and Life Action Plans

1. What would you like your work life and personal life to be like in *10 years time?*

Your work/career

Type of job
_____

Type of organisation
_____

Location
_____

Salary
_____

Your personal life

Relationship/family
situation
_____

Type of home/social
environment
_____

Valuation and location
of dwelling
_____

Type of social activities
and life
_____

2. Now be more specific and list your *specific goals* associated with your 10-year plan, e.g. Company Director of the firm you now work for, starting a family; or *general goals*, such

as living in the country; or even goals which are more a *set of criteria*, such as a job which involves a lot of people contact, or taking up music and learning to play a musical instrument.

10-Year Action Plan/Goals
Your work/career   *Your personal life*

_____   _____

_____   _____

_____   _____

_____   _____

3. Now list your career and personal goals in *order of priority*, and for each goal list activities required to enable you to attain that goal. Try and give yourself a target date and remember to ask yourself what things are likely to hinder the attainment of your goals and what can be done to utilise the helping agents and reduce the hindering ones:

10-Year Action Plan; Goals, Activities and Target Dates

Your work/career	*Target date*	*Your personal life*	*Target date*
Goal 1		Goal 1	
Activities		Activities	
Goal 2		Goal 2	
Activities		Activities	

Your work/career	Target date	Your personal life	Target date
Goal 3		Goal 3	
Activities		Activities	
Goal 4		Goal 4	
Activities		Activities	

4. Now repeat exercises 1, 2, and 3 formulating your:
   (i) 5-year career and personal life plan
   (ii) 1-year career and personal life plan
   (iii) 6-month career and personal life plan
   Your 1-year and 6-month plans will contain actions which can be taken *almost immediately*.

5. Do not forget that goals and action plans can always be revised and modified. Having formulated your four time-period plans, carefully review your goals and ask yourself the two following questions:
   (i) Are my goals worth attaining?
   (ii) Do I want to modify any of the action strategies I will need to take?

Career planning strategies can also be applied to the skills involved in becoming an effective manager. These are not only related to how well you do your job, but also to how you mould your career progression, how and when you take risks, gaining confidence and assertion, knowing the right time to move on from one job to another and so on.

It is often assumed that men and women have very different career patterns, and that women are not as mobile as men. However, in a recent study I carried out (with Cary Cooper) of nearly 1,000 men and women at all levels of management in Britain, what was particularly interesting in terms of job demographics and career-pattern demographics, were the *similarities* between the female and male managers. The majority of men and women had tended to have continuous work-pattern profiles, although a higher percentage of women had had a break from the workforce, and more female managers had at some time worked part-time. Both female and male managers shared the same average 8.4 years in full-time employment in their present organisation, and both had been an average of five years in their present job. Similarities in career- and job-mobility patterns were further confirmed by the findings that both female and male managers had worked for an average 3.7 companies/organisations. These results suggest that women in management have surprisingly similar job-change patterns to their male counterparts.

We also found that conflict over job mobility can be a problem for both men and women. More and more women committed to careers don't want to move because of their husbands' jobs, and similarly some men find their wives' careers hamper their own mobility (an issue I will be discussing in more depth in Chapter 7). Organisations have got to stop placing so much importance on a manager's mobility, and men and women should be able to receive promotion without being required to move, and thus remove the domestic and career dilemma of having to place one spouse's career before the other's.

It seems appropriate to end this chapter with the Career Planning Strategies compiled by Nikki Fonda, a former director of the Brunel University Management Programme. Nikki has highlighted some of the major vital ingredients which make up an effective manager and her/his subsequent career progression and development. The job requires confidence, good inter-personal skills – someone who is good at dealing with people and forming relationships – in other words, a person who has *good communication skills.*

Career planning strategies

Senior managers say that effective managers:

- Do not just take orders without discussion and without challenging them.

- In discussions with their boss, present their own views and constructive proposals for actions to be taken.

- Are honest with the boss about what is going on even if the news is not all good.

- Accept responsibility for errors of judgement or mistakes in their departments.

- Praise subordinates when they do well, and take corrective action when they do not come up to scratch.

- Go away and do things without constantly checking back, but ask for advice and help when they do not know what to do or are confused.

- Ensure that their subordinates understand clearly what their jobs and responsibilities are.

- Help their staff develop their capabilities.

- Defend and pursue their department's interests, but not to the exclusion of the interest of the business as a whole.

- Delegate work to their staff and do not try to do it all themselves.

What, in summary, is the effective manager doing?

He or she is *communicating*, and communicating in ways that don't put off other people, but do get on with the task and help to lead to a desirable outcome.

He or she is also communicating in ways that reinforce the self-respect of *both* parties to that communication.

Compiled by Nikki Fonda from her research, in Ryan and Fritchie *Career/ Life Planning Workshops for Women Managers*, Bristol Polytechnic/Manpower Services Commission, 1982, and reproduced here with permission

SUMMARY

- Choose the area of management you would like to work in with care by getting as much factual information as possible about the different options. Use careers advisory services and write to appropriate bodies for further information.

- Do not allow yourself to be steered into traditional female management fields unless you have decided specifically that that is the type of management career you wish to pursue. Also, beware of accepting new management job-title positions, which in reality have limited career advancement prospects.

- Make sure you choose the right subjects and gain the correct qualifications necessary for entry into your chosen management field. It is never too late to commence study, whether for 'O' levels or a degree course, and as a mature student work experience, etc may act as entry qualifications for certain courses (including degree courses).

- Whatever your study/qualification course, ensure that you are fully aware of the course curriculum and never be afraid to use the personal approach in order to gain a place on a particular course.

- Keep in mind that talent, ability and ambition alone can be a recipe for succeeding in your chosen management career.

- Make long- and short-term career/life plans, keeping in mind that they are flexible and can be modified.

- A list of useful addresses is given at the back of the book.

CHAPTER 3

Breaking Down the Barriers

'An old Hebrew tradition holds that this first creation included a female called Lillith. She was the very first defender of the cause of women's liberation. When Adam told Lillith that she was to obey his wishes, she replied: "We are equal; we are made of the same earth." So saying she flew up into the air and transformed herself into a demon who ate children. Even that early, women who would not subjugate themselves to the will of men were seen as witches.'

Sheldon Kopp, *If You Meet the Buddha on the Road, Kill Him!*, 1974

It is important to be aware of the best possible strategies for breaking down any initial barriers which may hamper your long-term career prospects. Obviously, all individuals, whether male or female, face hurdles and restrictions along their career paths. What I've attempted to do in this chapter is to concentrate on some of these potential hurdles which, as a member of a minority group in a male-dominated profession, may be of particular relevance to you: namely, the job application and interview stage; getting the management training you deserve; and the transition from secretary to manager. Finally, I have covered another route which more and more women are taking as a way of breaking into management – i.e. setting up their own business and becoming a female entrepreneur.

Job applications and interviews – how to be successful

Once you've decided on the type of job you'd like to do, you are faced with a number of ways of seeking such a job, including going to an employment agency, getting your name listed on the Professional and Executive Register (PER), answering advertisements, or approaching a company direct 'on spec'. This last approach is one which requires a certain amount of confidence and bravado and tends to be used the least often. But finding out the name of the appropriate person to write to and inquiring about possible job opportunities in their organisation (enclosing your curriculum vitae), often proves fruitful, especially if you make the effort to approach several companies. It shows initiative. The best line of approach is to suggest you go and meet the person at a convenient date and time. Such a meeting brings in the personal interaction and contact which is so important, and you will have, in fact, initiated an informal interview for yourself!

Following on from this, never ever be put off from using personal contacts in order to help yourself get a job. It's a fact of life that, especially as you go higher up the professional ladder, the majority of jobs are gained through personal contacts and recommendations, as well as through individuals being approached and asked to apply for certain positions – i.e. being 'head hunted'. Even with the advantage of a personal contact, you can never be certain about getting the job, but it most definitely helps.

Regardless of the method used, you will almost certainly be required to prepare a letter of application and your curriculum vitae (CV). It is of vital importance that these are of a good standard, as emphasised by Sarah, who has a responsible job as an Area Manager and wide experience of both interviewing prospective employees and being interviewed for job positions herself:

'It never ceases to amaze me how women tend to undersell themselves on their CVs and at interviews compared to men. With the job market being what it is, you have got to present a good CV and covering letter if you want it to stand out from the many others. It should be typed and concise and to the point and include job descriptions, responsibilities, numbers responsible for, sums of money involved and also details about your hobbies and interests – I know of one woman who was given a management job in a large male-dominated organisation mainly because she had a pilot's licence!

When I now apply for a job (including internal positions) I have a set routine which seems to be quite successful. Firstly I try to find out as much about the job content and the interviewers as possible. This isn't as difficult as it sounds and women need to make use of network systems in order to make it easier. If I find that the job is below my qualifications and status and current salary, then I don't apply. If I am still interested, after carefully preparing my curriculum vitae, I then begin to prepare for the interview itself. I make a list of possible questions which may be asked during the interview and also include some questions which I can ask the interviewer/s, as they always ask at the end of the interview if you have any questions and it doesn't look good if you haven't. Then, I find a willing friend and get them to role-play the whole interview with me using the possible questions I've prepared. This enables me actually to rehearse the responses I may give and to modify them accordingly.'

Your job application letter and curriculum vitae

Your letter of application should be concise, short and well laid out; if at all possible it ought to be typed. Overleaf is a sample letter which illustrates the correct layout. It's important to include your telephone number. If you begin by addressing the person by name, e.g. 'Mr Y', then end the letter 'Yours sincerely'; otherwise, if it's 'Dear sir or madam' end 'Yours faithfully'.

Although personally I'm an advocate of the term 'Ms', I suggest that until attitudes become more enlightened, don't refer to yourself as 'Ms' in your application as quite a number of personnel officers (male and female) have told me they immediately label the woman as a militant feminist and potential trouble maker!

3 Cross Street,
London NW3.

5th July 1985

Telephone: 01-123 9876

Mr John Cox,
Senior Personnel Manager,
James, Davies and Shipton Fabrics,
56–60 Swallow Road,
London SW15.

Dear Mr Cox,

I am very interested in applying for the position of Marketing Manager which you advertised in today's *Guardian*, as I feel I may be well suited for the job.

As you will see from my enclosed curriculum vitae, I have had a series of posts in a number of different firms, starting as a personal assistant in a market research company and working my way up to Assistant Marketing Manager in my present job with Ross Textiles. During my two years here as part of the marketing team, we have increased our market share by 30%, as well as raising our corporate profile.

I have recently completed a part-time refresher course at the London Business School, specialising in marketing. I should be happy to make myself available for interview during normal business hours. I look forward to hearing from you in the near future.

Yours sincerely,

Christine Cook

In your letter you will need to mention where you saw the advertisement and explain briefly why you think you would be suitable for the job. Include any relevant educational, professional qualifications and training, as well as previous work experience.

Of equal importance is your CV. In a series of articles in *The Guardian*, Virginia Burdon quoted the following advice from consultant Jean Harvey of the Professional and Executive Register:

> 'Your curriculum vitae is your life. Experience, Attitudes, Knowledge, Skills, all on one piece of paper. It's your advertisement; it's got to convince someone to see you in a 30-second glance...
>
> '... Never lie, although it's O.K. to disguise dicey facts. Telephone numbers? Always put in the local and national codes to feed any impulse to pick up the phone and say you're on. And if you're a woman, disguise your sex by using initials only when applying for a 'man's' job.
>
> 'Marital status? Forget about it if you're divorced. Skip the kids. And if you're over 35, put down the date of your birth only.'
>
> *The Guardian*, Feb. 9, 1983, p.16

To get an idea of the way to formulate your CV, turn to the final chapter in this book in which five successful women managers describe their work and personal experiences and views, each preceded by their own CV. As a final resort you can always pay to get your CV compiled and typed professionally (these service agencies often advertise in the higher quality newspapers and professional journals).

The job interview

On the whole, interviewers for middle and senior management posts are likely to be senior and/or personnel managers, who tend to be male. Junior management and graduate selection tends to involve personnel and middle management interviewers, and again the majority are male although there is more likelihood of female interviewers being involved. There has been a lot of research in the past few years analysing the qualities sought in a job applicant for management positions. Interestingly, *personality* factors are generally regarded as more important than experience, intelligence or qualifications. The qualities most commonly sought are 'contribution to the job', 'motivation', and 'ability to get on with colleagues' (British Institute of Management, 1980). You should keep this in mind if you have any misgivings about being under-qualified.

Unfortunately though, it is still a fact of life that women often start at an inherent disadvantage at the management selection interview stage. In 1975 a study by Hunt found that managers thought that all the qualities needed for managerial jobs were more likely to be found in men than in women, and a more recent follow-up study in 1979 by McIntosh discovered that although attitudes had become slightly more favourable, women were still regarded as inferior. Thus, careful preparation both at the application stage and pre-interview stage is essential.

Prepare yourself in advance by finding out as much about the company and the job as you can. Make a list of the possible questions you may be asked during the interview, including queries about your personal life and domestic arrangements. Try and arrange a 'dummy' interview with someone you trust. Make sure you have a number of questions to ask your interviewer at the end of the interview. Besides details regarding the job *per se*, you may wish to inquire about your contract of employment, pension schemes, fringe benefits (such as expense accounts, company cars, etc), and, most important, what the prospects are for promotion and training on the job.

Finally, the question of salary will be mentioned and this is when you make sure that you don't accept a salary below that which your age, qualifications and experience warrant. If there are quibbles over your pay, unless the job is a newly-formed position it may well be worth inquiring as to the salary given to your predecessor (especially if that person was male!).

Sheila Rothwell of the Henley Management College presented some important advice to prospective women managers during the interview at a workshop she ran at the European Seminar on Practical Approaches to Women's Management

Development, organised by the European Foundation for Management Development (EFMD) in Brussels, in 1983. Below is a summary of some of the main points she highlighted:

1. Candidates need consciously to relax (and remember the need to put a nervous male interviewer at ease).

2. Project a positive, professional and confident image. It is useful to give an impression of initiative and energy but important not to dominate.

3. Women need to check that their voice is pitched low, if possible, as a high voice tends to appear less authoritative (especially in comparison with a man) and nervousness tends to make the voice rise.

4. Eye-contact should not be overdone (for its sexual connotations) and it is sometimes better to switch to the mouth.

5. Smiling is acceptable; giggling is not (female laughter is usually described as 'giggling').

6. On the whole, candidates need to tell interviewers what they want to hear – but briefly. Nervous candidates often talk too much, bore the interviewer or more significantly blunt the impact of what they have to say. The aim must be to convey concise and clear evidence of competence and career commitment.

Combating interview discrimination

The 1975 Sex Discrimination Act made it unlawful for anyone to discriminate against you because of your sex, or, in the employment field, because you are married. The areas covered include education, goods, training bodies and trade unions, facilities and services. Undoubtedly, many women feel that they are discriminated against (directly or indirectly) during the interview stage, and management interviews are no exception as this 27-year-old woman found out:

'I recently attended an interview for a Head of Section job. I am married and have no children and my husband has a good job in industry. It shocked me though, as almost half the interview was taken up with the interviewers (all male) asking me questions about my husband and his job! I was beginning to think that it was he who had applied for the job and not me, and he isn't even the same discipline. They also gave me the impression that they thought it unlikely that I would be willing to commute such a distance even though as a dual career couple we have had to live apart during the week while I lived in rented accommodation, due to my job being based over 50 miles away from my husband's work. I emphasised that both our careers were just as important but I think they envisaged me leaving to have a family eventually, even though we've decided not to have children. On reflection I should have stopped the interview and made my feelings clear, asking calmly what relevance questions about my husband had. The problem is you feel vulnerable during an interview, especially if you want the job badly. However, if the interviewers are like that, it makes you wonder what it's going to be like as a woman working in that type of organisation.'

If after an interview you feel that you have been discriminated against, it's a good idea to take notes on what was said straight away. This will be invaluable in raising the matter with your union and if necessary in making a complaint under the Sex Discrimination Act. (If you are not a member of a union you can seek advice from the EOC or the National Council for Civil Liberties.) A complaint of discrimination in employment opportunities under the Sex Discrimination Act must be made to an Industrial Tribunal within three months of the act complained of being committed. This period may be extended if it is just and equitable to do so.

There are several ways of combating at least some of the barriers you may face at the application and interview stage. These are described by three of the women managers I spoke to:

Never give up
'I believe that women have got to learn to face rejection at interviews and "never give up"; you have to persevere and

not let the whole thing get you down. I went to six interviews before I was finally offered a Deputy Headship, and the final interview was the only one when I wasn't asked what kind of childcare facilities I had for my sons – they are 15 and 17 years of age by the way!'

Let your childcare arrangements and future plans be known
'Women should, I feel, bring up the subject of childcare, mobility, husbands, future plans regarding a family, etc in a firm but calm way to their interviewers, stating that they will not interfere with the way you do your job and that you hope they will not be taking them into account because you are female. Indeed, you can also point out that this would be unlawful under the Sex Discrimination Act. Just because the interviewers don't ask you such questions, it should never be assumed that they are not in the backs of their minds, so it's better to clarify the situation yourself. My husband was recently on the board of a management selection committee. The only female interviewee was by far the best candidate for the job. She was 42 years old and divorced. However, the dilemma for the board concerning her appointment was to do with "the fact that she was a very attractive woman and would bound to get married again and therefore might not stay in the job long" . . . She didn't get the job.'

Dressing for the part
'Being a woman in management, you are highly visible and dress is important, especially at the interview stage. Whether we like it or not, women are judged on their appearance much more than men are. For interviews, I always try and present a feminine, business-like appearance. Trying to be "butch" or sexy in any way is definitely not on. I recently had an important internal interview for the big step for women managers – the transition from upper middle to senior management. I knew my boss would be on the panel but I made a special effort both in preparation and dress. When I walked into the interview room, my boss immediately said "Did you buy that new suit especially for the interview?" He seemed rather surprised

but I'm sure it illustrated to him how seriously I took the whole procedure. I'd also recently got married and so I made it clear that even if I did decide to have a family in the future, I would only be taking maternity leave and that my career was very important ... I got the job and am now the youngest woman in our organisation ever to have reached senior management.'

Making the most of management training schemes

Once you've secured a suitable job position, making sure you get the right amount and type of management training you need is vital to your career development and prospects. Numerous studies in this country have found that many women find it difficult to persuade their firms to send them on training courses and one way of resolving this is to pay to go on courses yourself, as this Production Manager explained:

'I have found this company unwilling to send me on management (as opposed to technical) training, or on courses specifically for women managers, where problems that women managers experience might be dealt with and discussed.

'I have paid for and attended two of The Industrial Society Saturday development courses. These have been of tremendous benefit to me because it is a great relief to meet other women managers and find that they have exactly the same problems. I feel less of a freak – I'm not imagining it all. I also feel less isolated – there are other women managers out there somewhere!'

From my own experience of talking to male managers and personnel officers, the common excuse for not sending people on training courses is once again linked to the recession and 'hard times':

'My company cannot afford to send people on many internal or external training courses, and job-related courses take priority over inter-personal skills training, etc. Also, with staff cutbacks, we often can't afford to lose someone for days or even weeks.'

Interestingly, the 'You're too valuable for us to let you be away from your job' line, is often used on women managers as an excuse for not sending them on management courses (as well as for not promoting women!). Women managers, especially at junior level, benefit greatly from inter-personal skills training, as described by one female middle manager:

'I strongly feel that the training required for women entering management areas should be centred not only on the specific skills for the job in question, but also on the essential theme that they are entering a "man's world", and in order to compete on equal terms must develop a mental attitude that gives them the confidence to deal with senior male managers on equal terms. I am not suggesting that they should relinquish their outward feminine appearance, but they cannot expect to rely on tears or any other feminine wiles to overcome difficult problems or situations.'

Indeed, my own research with Cary Cooper confirmed these assumptions. When asked 'What type of training do you need?', the response from the 60 female managers interviewed supported the contention that bases of social skill training were in the areas of confidence building, and learning to be assertive (see Table 3.1).

This lack of confidence (to be discussed in detail in Chapter 5) can act as a barrier for women when it comes to getting the training they deserve, as illustrated by this young administrative assistant:

'I have mechanical interests and would like to go on more engineering courses rather than administrative ones, but I don't have the confidence or push. Like many women I know, I decided to try and go it alone and show initiative so I asked my manager if the company would sponsor me to do an Open University degree in Arts and Technology. He said he thought I'd have no chance so my request didn't even get as far as Personnel. I thought "blow it", I'll do it off my own bat. I felt gunned down though. What I should have done, of course, is to have been persistent and even gone to Personnel myself. As women we have got to learn to fight for our rights.'

Table 3.1 *The female managers interview sample: The training we need*

Type of training	% of total sample
Confidence building	50%
Assertion skills	42%
Inter-personal skills	12%
General management skills including delegation, disciplining, negotiating	10%
Learning to cope with men at work including sex role stereotyping imposition	8%
Political awareness	7%
Training for men to cope with women	6%
Desocialising *re*: sex stereotyping	5%
Leadership	5%
Retraining for women entering workforce	3%
Personal presentation	3%
Power of speech and public speaking	3%
Resilience	2%
How to do well at interviews	2%

Source: Marilyn Davidson and Cary Cooper, *Stress and the Woman Manager* and *Women Managers: Their Problems and What can be done To Help Them*, 1983

Certainly, *it is your right* to make sure you get the management training – either on internal or external courses – that you require in order to attain the skills and experiences you need to succeed in your particular area. Many of the women managers I interviewed said they had benefited more by attending 'off-company' courses, where they were able to share work experience problems with people from different organisations as opposed to being constrained within the context of an 'in-company' training programme. Imogen is a senior area manager in the catering industry, is in her late twenties and earns over £15,000 a year. She gave some invaluable advice about management training strategies for women:

'Like a lot of women managers, compared to my male colleagues I have had to fight and be more persistent with my bosses (who have all been male) about being allowed to attend training courses. From my own experiences I would give other women the following advice:

1. Sit down and analyse exactly which skills – business, technical or personal - you need to develop.

2. Having isolated these, find out what courses your colleagues and superiors have been on (particularly males) and make sure that you also include those on your list.

3. Put the skills you most need to develop in order of priority and see which courses are listed in your company training manual. These will often exclude specific inter-personal skills training in areas dealing specifically with women managers, and information about such courses can be found by contacting such bodies as the MSC Training Division and The Industrial Society.

4. You have got to learn *never to give up* with your requests to go on training courses. I have often been refused with the age-old excuse "we're too busy, we can't spare you Imogen, job experience is what counts, etc." Then I looked round and saw my male colleagues going on training courses I was missing out on. I pointed this out to my boss and made a strong, firm issue out of it (knowing full well he really thought that it was a waste of time sending women on training courses as they would be eventually leaving to have babies anyway). From that day I refused ever to be put off, and if a request was refused I required the reason and would make it clear I would be asking again, *and soon*. Point out what *the company can gain* by sending you on a particular course as well as your own individual needs – the aim is to get a balance.

5. Finally, if you still are not getting the same training opportunities as your male colleagues, my advice is to leave and get a job with a company with more enlightened attitudes. As well, there is no harm in going on

weekend training courses and financing yourself or
gaining extra qualifications at evening classes.'

Taking advantage of management development programmes for women

The Sex Discrimination Act of 1975 makes provision in
Sections 47 and 48 for 'positive discrimination' in training,
and since women managers still form a small percentage of
managers in the UK, management training and development
certainly meet the Act's criteria. However, in my experience,
women, especially those who have firmly established their
management careers, are often strongly opposed to all-women
training courses. In an interview sample of 60 women
managers, 22% were absolutely against female-only training
courses of any kind, believing them to be a form of discrimination via segregation, arguing that it was too unlike the 'real
world' of organisations. Nevertheless, the majority of this
sample conceded that all-female management training courses
probably had benefits, especially for women just beginning a
career in management (most of the women also believed that
they would have benefited personally).

Many women have found women-only courses to be of great
use to them and they shouldn't be dismissed out of hand. In an
article written by Dr Mike Smith in the MSC *Women and
Training News*, entitled 'Management development programme at UMIST' he quoted the following comment from
one of the women participants who was Chief Sub-Editor with
Time Life Books:

'I was initially somewhat sceptical of going on a course
specifically aimed at women but found it increasingly
interesting and am looking forward to the third week. I
found particularly useful the opportunity to take a hard look
at my present job and my career generally. The different
aspects of management presented has been varied, with
copious follow-up material which is to the point and useful.
The exercises, films and role-playing are in addition good
fun and the "homework" projects provide a practical link
between the three weeks.

'Inevitably not all parts of the course are equally relevant to everyone. Overt sex discrimination is prevalent in some industries more than others. For instance, I am one of an editorial management team of six women and two men. However, biased society and family conditioning does mean that self-assertion training is essential to most of us.'

Management development courses for women are being run by the Manpower Services Commission throughout the country and include career/life planning workshops, training for women returners, engineering/information technology courses and a number of self-development courses. The MSC are also involved in schemes aimed at helping women into industry at management level. For example, recently the MSC and the Hotel and Catering Industry Training Board gave grants of £1,250 to 35 women for one-year in-service (with external courses) development programmes to help women into the industry at management level. Also, as part of MSC's New Training Initative, the Open Tech Programme is aimed at employed and unemployed adults (both men and women), and training projects cover a wide range of areas and industries.

A useful publication which reports news about women's training courses and other related issues is the bi-monthly MSC *Women and Training News*. It is a free publication and you can become a regular recipient by writing to the Editor. Other bodies who specialise in women's development courses include a number of independent consultants, the National Organisation for Women's Management Education (NOWME), The Industrial Society and *Cosmopolitan*.

Rachel Shattock is the Courses Organiser for *Cosmopolitan* and she described to me the content and feel of the various courses they offer:

'We are introducing new courses all the time and our regular courses include Career Planning, such as the Saturday Development course, Putting Yourself Across, Setting up Your Own Business, Getting out of the Secretarial Trap, Micro-Computer Course and Careers in Computing. We also run Media, Radio and Television Workshops, Political Workshops backed by the 300 Group, and Life Skills which include Assertiveness Workshops and a Fulfilment Day.

'The courses aren't all-female by design! Most of our courses are open to both sexes, it's just rare that we get men booking. Assertiveness and Saturday Development are female-only because they tackle issues pertinent to women only and it is also felt that the absence of men promotes a completely free exchange of ideas. The 300 Group courses are also women-only because they are part of a particular campaign to get more women into parliament.

'We get very good feedback from the courses. We have recently introduced some post-course questionnaires so that we can monitor the response and look for improvements. An unfavourable comment is a very rare occurrence indeed.'

From secretary to manager – How to step through the barrier

Do *not* go into secretarial work as a route to a career in management. One has to be realistic and acknowledge that the days when it was relatively easy to break away from the secretarial role into professional and management jobs are largely over. This is even the case in organisations such as the BBC in which the secretarial route was an accepted path for potential women researchers and producers to follow. Surprisingly, an 11-year follow-up study investigating the changing role of secretaries in Central London by Rosalie Silverstone and Rosemary Towler (of the City University Business School), found that in 1981 secretarial work had still been chosen by some as a job offering a stepping stone into non-secretarial careers. However, in reality, about 60% of secretaries believed they had absolutely no promotion prospects in their present jobs, and four out of five secretaries who had taken up secretarial work because they saw it as a stepping stone were now in dead end jobs. Only very few secretaries felt they had any opportunity to go into other fields, and for the majority with promotion prospects it meant working for a person with higher status.

A most interesting finding by the researchers was that when

employers were asked if there were any jobs in their organisation into which secretaries might move, given appropriate support and training, *two-thirds* named such openings and opportunities (see Table 3.2).

Table 3.2 *A selection of alternative jobs for secretaries which were mentioned by employers*

Account Executive	Futures Market Trader
Accountant	Legal Executive
Accounting Assistant	Life Assistant (Insurance)
Accounts Manager	Manager
Actuary	Marketing Administrator
Administrator	Personnel Officer
Assistant Bursar	Press Officer
Bank Clerk	Programmer
Bookkeeper	PR Executive
Broker	Sales Person
Cashier	Social Worker
Clerical Officer	Surveyor
Dental Assistant	Travel Clerk
Director	Typesetter
Draughtsman	Word Processor Co-ordinator
Film Producer	Word Processor Operator

Source: Rosalie Silverstone and Rosemary Towler, *Secretarial Work in Central London 1970–1981*, MSC, 1983

My own interviews with scores of secretaries in a large multinational company confirmed many of these findings. Many secretaries did want to branch into non-secretarial jobs and careers, and the most dissatisfied and frustrated women were those with the highest educational qualifications – indeed, I interviewed typists with nine 'O' levels and three 'A' levels! But, like the City University Business School study, although many managers believed that there were opportunities for secretaries to go into other jobs, most thought that the majority of secretaries were happy being secretaries even though, according to the women themselves, this was often not the case. Clearly, secretaries often lack the initiative and confidence to let their ambitions be known.

Therefore, based on the findings of these studies, if you are a secretary, clerk or administrative supervisor, etc and you wish to break into another work area with more prospects and management potential, there are certain courses of action open to you:

1. Identify which job you would like to aspire to (this is easier if your organisation is small but if you work in a large organisation make efforts to find out what jobs are available in other departments and sections).

2. Approach your employer in order to explore the feasibility of transferring, going on relevant training courses, etc.

3. If you feel you lack confidence about going to your employer, get support from colleagues and practise what you are going to say with a supportive friend. Remember you have *nothing to lose* and plenty to gain and you may well be pleasantly surprised. Don't give up though, persistence shows determination and ambition.

4. If it becomes obvious that you have no chance of moving away from secretarial work in your organisation (the City University Business School study, for example, found that opportunities were much slimmer in professional offices, especially if the secretary did not have basic qualifications such as 'A' levels or a degree), do not be afraid to apply for jobs in other organisations which will be more sympathetic to your career goals. I know of one woman who recently applied for a secretarial position in a large organisation and during the interview made it clear that she eventually wanted to switch from secretarial to commerce. She was immediately offered a commercial apprenticeship and has left her typewriter behind for good.

From Secretary to Press Officer – A personal account
'When I was a secretary, I made sure that my bosses were aware of my ambitions to get out of secretarial, my qualifications, and any part-time studies I was taking. I would also try and be more of a PA for them rather than just a secretary, this way not only did I get more varied job experience learning more about the company but it also

enabled me to show my skills. I have had knock-backs (including being forced to return to secretarial work at one stage) but you have got to pick yourself up and keep trying. It's important to make yourself and your ambitions known and to get as much exposure in the company as possible.

'I was able to get out of secretarial work as I looked for opportunities and took them. I had a manager who encouraged me and I used personal contacts to get on – I saw that was the way managers progressed – using the "old boy" network. You have also got to be selective in the jobs you are willing to go into. I was once offered a job in Office Furniture Management but I refused as it offered no chance of promotion. I found out later that it was a job they had created especially for me. Even though you have secretarial roots, you've got to plan your career and assess the career prospects of each job you go into.'

The female entrepreneur – Setting up your own business

Another way of breaking down the barriers and stepping into management is to start your own business. Unfortunately there are no official statistics on the proportion of UK small firms which are owned and controlled by women, and the only related figures we have are from 1975 when about 4% of economically active females and 9% of males were registered as self-employed. However, if American trends are anything to go by, this figure is on the increase. A recent US report on the state of small business says that as far as women-owned businesses are concerned, their number increased by 33% between 1977 and 1980, with the most rapid growth in the non-traditional areas such as finance, insurance, real estate, manufacturing, agricultural services and mining.

Clive Woodcock, editor of the 'Small Business' section in *The Guardian*, points out that among the Government's famous 100 measures for small businesses there are no specific policy initiatives for minority-owned businesses, a description which is often taken to include women-owned businesses as well. On a brighter note, however, women are using the MSC Enterprise Allowance Scheme and setting up a range of businesses from engineering services, knitwear, video retail and calf rearing to becoming an estate agent and manufacturing electric alarms. (Details of this scheme can be obtained from the Manpower Services Commission.)

Managing your own business may be an attractive proposition if you have spent many years at home bringing up children and feel you lack qualifications. Clive Woodcock recently interviewed a woman named Mary Horner who did just that and decided to develop a new business based on what had been a family pastime for a number of years – that of inventing games:

> 'The games were usually invented by her husband, Joe, tax partner in a leading firm of accountants, and daughter Clare, with other members of the family playing and helping to refine the games.
>
> '"Joe tends to devise rather complex and demanding games and it is Clare who often develops them into games which can be played more widely. She does some testing of the market by seeing how friends at school react to them and comment on them," says Mrs Horner.
>
> 'Though she had never run a business before, she saw the opportunity which presented itself with a flow of games invented within the family which had a commercial potential. She set up a company called Noetic Pastimes, a name based on a Greek word associated with the workings of the brain appropriately for the challenging nature of some of the games planned . . .
>
> 'There are already several new games ready for widening the range of products offered by Noetic Pastimes as demand builds up and the company grows. In the meantime Mrs Horner is gathering sales experience the hard way – going through the doors of hundreds of shops in the greater Manchester area and honing the sales pitch direct to the retailers.'

'Cogitating on the games people play – Basing a business on a family pastime', *The Guardian*, Nov. 25, 1983, p. 22

One of the few projects investigating the position and needs (including training needs) of the female entrepreneur in this country is being sponsored by Shell UK under its Small Business initiative, and being carried out by Jean and David Watkins in the New Enterprise Centre at the University of Manchester Business School. They maintain that evidence from unofficial sources indicates that the proportion of businesses owned and controlled by women in the UK is now around 6% of the total. As part of their studies to ascertain the origins, backgrounds, characteristics, problems and successes of the current generation of women owner-managers, the Watkins surveyed a sample of 58 women running between them some 49 independent businesses. Listed below are some very interesting findings highlighting the profile of the typical female entrepreneur in their sample:

Parental background: She is some four times more likely to have had an entrepreneurial parent (father and/or mother) than a member of the general population.

Age at start of business: Compared to a control group of male entrepreneurs, females were younger when they started up their businesses. For men the average age was 39 years, for women it was 32.

Education: 19% of the women were educated to 'O' level, 10% to 'A' level and 26% had a degree or equivalent. As well, 19% had qualifications in commercial subjects at sub-degree level (secretarial courses, etc) and 26% had professional qualifications.

Work experience: Only 60% of the Watkins' sample of women were on their first business and no cases of outright failure were reported, although in some cases conscious decisions had been made to discontinue marginal or unprofitable businesses. On the whole, the subsequent ventures were normally both larger and more sophisticated businesses than previous ones. Half of the women had entered a business venture of which they had no direct prior experience without any managerial experience in a different business context, this compared with only 5% of men in their control group!

Career paths: The main reason for women deciding to start their own businesses was due to a strong motivation for autonomy and achievement, which had been frustrated by the women's previous training and background.

Problems: When asked to highlight the problems that they had encountered in running their own businesses, the women interviewed maintained that their most frequent problem was lack of business training, followed by obtaining finance, poor security for loans/special conditions, obtaining property, and demands of business affecting personal relationships.

Advice to women starting their own business

I asked Jean Watkins what sort of advice she would give to any woman who wanted to start her own business. She emphasised the following seven major points:

1. What kind of business?
Go for something you know and understand:
- Preferably choose something in which you have relevant work experience or educational background.
- You may have a particular hobby you could turn into a business.

However, recent research has shown that determined women can actually succeed even when they have no previous experience of the particular trade they are entering and often don't have any managerial experience at all.

2. Customers
Always start with your market:
- Make sure you can identify customers.
- Don't assume that because you like making particular products or because you have a particular service to offer that people will necessarily want to buy it or use it.
- This is an area you will need to research and if possible get firm orders before going into production/service.

3. Partners
- Starting on your own can be lonely and a *well-balanced* partnership is more likely to succeed than somebody starting on his/her own.

- In a partner you should look for somebody with complementary skills to your own, *not* people with identical skills and interests. For example, if you are best at production look for a partner who is good at dealing with customers.

4. Risk reduction

- Try to start with as little risk as possible. If you can start your business easily from home don't take on the commitment of business premises until you are sure that the business really needs them.

5. Bankers

- Make sure that when you do borrow money you borrow sufficient – it's very difficult to go back for more until the business has proved its worth.
- In general women can have a harder time borrowing money because they are less likely to have a track record and less likely to have security. However, when a woman does present a really well-documented business proposal to a bank manager it is often unusual enough to warrant a sympathetic hearing.
- Don't forget banks are in business to lend money. They are not doing you a favour – they need to lend money to make profits, so shop around until you find what you want at the right price.

6. Professional advice

- Take as much professional advice as you can when starting up.
- Lots of free advice is available from local enterprise and government small firms services. Freephone 2444.
- Regrettably few women apply for the many free enterprise training courses sponsored by MSC and some independent bodies, though those who do seem to do particularly well. Contact local MSC area offices for provision in your area.

7. Books and information

Two books which are particularly useful:

- *Small Business Kit* by D. S. Watkins *et al*, published by the

National Extension College. This book is particularly helpful for working through and developing your own business ideas.

- *The Small Business Guide* by Colin Barrow, published by the BBC. This book offers sources of information for new and small businesses.

SUMMARY

- Take care and time over the preparation of your job application letter and curriculum vitae and do not undersell yourself. Be concise and to the point.

- Never go to an interview under-prepared. Find out as much about the job and organisation as possible. List probable questions you might be asked, and also assumptions concerning your work and personal life which might be made by your interviewer/s. Rehearse a mock interview with a friend.

- 'If at first you don't succeed, try, try, try again!' Men also often get rejected at job interviews but tend to persevere with job applications more than women do – so never give up.

- Ensure you get the right amount and type of management training you deserve and require. In particular, do not fall behind your male colleagues. Take advantage of women management development courses.

- As a secretary (clerk or supervisor, etc) it is possible to break away from secretarial work and embark on a management career. Decide on the specific area of work/job you wish to transfer to and let your ambitions be known to your employer.

- If you decide to set up your own business, follow the advice given by the experts and don't be afraid to seek sponsorship in order to attend enterprise training courses.

CHAPTER 4

Being in the Minority – How to Cope

'I mean, what is a woman? I assure you, I do not know. I do not believe that you know. I do not believe that anybody can know until she has expressed herself in all the arts and professions open to human skill.'

Virginia Woolf, *Professions for Women* from *The Death Of The Moth And Other Essays*, 1942

Having embarked on your management career it is highly likely that you, as a woman, will be in the minority. Moreover, when women comprise less than 15% of a total category in an organisation, they can be labelled 'tokens', which means that they tend to be viewed as symbols of their group rather than as individuals. I am well aware that many women enjoy and thrive on the situation where most of their colleagues and superiors are male. Conversely, other women (especially those new to management) do experience additional pressures not felt by the dominant (male) members of the same organisational status, and these potential strains should be acknowledged and dealt with constructively. In this chapter I have isolated some of these major disadvantages, and have presented some positive coping strategies. The potential problem areas include feelings of isolation, high visibility, performance pressures, business travel, and entertaining.

Combating isolation

Results from my own research projects and interviews suggest that the female manager who is most likely to suffer feelings of isolation at work is the younger woman who is just starting her career and who has few, if any, female colleagues or superiors (i.e. role models) to whom she can look for support and advice. A young woman, just starting her career, explained how feeling isolated and missing other female colleagues affected her:

> 'I do feel isolated yes, as sometimes you would like to talk to another woman as an equal. The only other women I have to talk to are all subordinates and you can't unburden yourself to them to the same extent. It's not that you want their advice or anything, you just want to share the burden with them. You want to get it off your chest.'

Never put up with a situation where you feel this sort of isolation. There are ways of coping, as this senior female executive I interviewed illustrates:

> 'There have been times in the past when I felt real pangs of isolation and almost loneliness at work. I must say though it does get easier the higher you climb in the management hierarchy. As a woman you have got to blend in with the male conversation that's going on around you – if it's about cars, for example, then chip in about your own car, what happened last time you had it serviced, and so on. If you show you are willing to blend in with them, then the men will probably join in with the subjects you wish to talk about. I also have a few close women friends who are in similar management positions in other organisations and they act as very important support systems. We meet regularly and discuss work issues and problems, often it just helps to talk about it with a woman in a similar situation to yours. *You cannot survive if you isolate yourself.*'

Adopting a mentor

Another method which some women are developing in order to combat isolation (as well as to facilitate their own career development prospects) is the mentor/patron/boss situation, whereby a future manager is informally trained by her immediate superior. Having a mentor can be very important as he or she can help to develop the managerial skills of his or her female protegée by giving her progressively more difficult assignments and responsibilities.

As a trainee manager in a large organisation, Jane described how she first became aware of the mentor system by watching the behaviour of her male colleague:

'When I was training, I was one of the first women graduates they had employed and I did feel on my own and isolated. Like a lot of women, I tended not to highlight my successes to my boss but just assumed that he'd notice. I didn't tell him how ambitious I was either. I had one male colleague who was taken on at the same time as I was and I began to notice that whenever he met our boss either socially in the pub or in the office, he would make a point of letting the boss know how he was doing as well as his hopes for the future. Eventually, the boss took him under his wing and he was promoted before I was. Since then I have adopted the very same policy with my bosses and it has worked very well for me. I've had a series of mentors throughout my career, and besides helping me and my being able to learn from them, many have become close friends and allies; and in a world as a lone woman, that's a tremendous asset.'

Like Jane, I have found that the majority of women managers in this country have had at least one or two mentors, (usually male although not exclusively so), who have given them special help and support which facilitated their advancement. Nevertheless, it is interesting to note that some writers on management subjects believe that the notion that mentors are important to a woman's career development has been over-emphasised and that the popularity of the mentor concept tends to reinforce the male-dominated organisational *status quo*. My response is that women should, whenever possible, take advantage of the mentor system, and once they get into power situations they too can and *should* adopt their own protegées.

Forming support networks

Young men going into management are soon made members of that exclusive club, 'The Old Boy Network'. However, as a woman in management, the task of breaking into this male-dominated 'club' can prove difficult and one is denied social support, contacts, opportunities and policy information. Indeed, it has been estimated that over 50% of all jobs in management come through personal contacts. A young stock-broker trainee, who was the first woman they had ever appointed in that firm in such a position, described how her total exclusion from the old boy network had affected her:

> 'The men I worked with treated me like some sort of "pet". They would say "Oh, we mustn't say that in front of . . ." It made no difference when I told them I didn't mind, and I felt very isolated. They would go to their all-male clubs at lunchtime, and that of course is where a lot of the real business goes on and I was excluded from it. It would have been much easier if there had been another woman in my position, someone to talk to, to get support from.'

In fact, in this country there is a growing movement, originating from the United States, advocating networking for women in the professions. More and more professional bodies are setting up their own network systems which have a career/job/female bias. Besides the network organisations I have mentioned, such as the National Association for Women's Management Education (NOWME) and Women in Management, numerous other women's groups have formed, and listed below is a random selection to give an idea of the range of support groups one can join:

The Academic Women's Achievement Group
The AWAG is concerned with the under-representation of women in Universities and is comprised of women academics as well as academic-related women such as administrative, senior technical, library and computer staff.

The British Association of Women Executives
The British Association was founded in 1954 and is affiliated to *Les Femmes Chefs d'Enterprises Mondiales*, an international

organisation comprising 14 member countries including Greece, Italy, Canada and France. The main aim of the Association is to bring together professional women who own, or control, an industry, a company or a business house, whether they operate alone or with co-directors.

The Fawcett Society
An organisation which has been a campaigner for equality between the sexes since 1866. It works through sub-committees of its members who have special interests and expert knowledge of employment, education and public affairs.

Federation of Business and Professional Women
The UK Federation has some 400 clubs and it hopes to form clubs in every district where there is potential. Its aims are to promote a free and responsible society in which women take an active part in decision-making at all levels; to determine, work for, and maintain fair opportunities in education and training, and to encourage co-operation and foster understanding among women throughout the world.

Focus
This is a recent non-profit making organisation, started by a group of women living in London who felt there was a need for a centre providing a clearing house of information relating to local services, schools, childcare and community organisations; and to offer information and guidance on educational and career opportunities; and to be used as a meeting place for people with similar interests.

International Toastmistress Clubs
An international organisation which trains women (and men) to have confidence in all forms of speaking, from polishing up conversation skills to addressing large crowds.

Network
An organisation for executive and professional women in commerce, industry and the arts; enabling women from different occupations to exchange experiences and build up contacts with others whom they might not ordinarily meet.

Women in Industry
Originally formed by a small group of women employed by

Phillips who felt the need to support and be supported as women in a predominately male environment. Members represent the banking, petroleum, printing, food and other industries as well as academia and a growing self-employed category.

Zonta International
A world-wide service organisation of professional and business women. Its aims are to encourage high ethical standards in business and the professions; to improve the political, legal and professional status of women; and to work towards the advancement of understanding, goodwill and peace through a world fellowship of women in business and the professions.

Addresses of all these groups are listed at the back of the book. There are also a host of women's network groups catering specifically for women members of particular professions and industries, for example:

Association of Personal Assistants and Secretaries
Association of Women in Enterprise
Association of Women in Public Relations
The Association of Women Solicitors
British Women Pilots' Association
The Executive Secretaries Association
Institute of Qualified Private Secretaries
National Association of Women Pharmacists
The Women's Advertising Club of London
Women in Banking
Women in the Civil Service
Women and Computing
The Women's Engineering Society
Women's Film, Television and Video Network
Women in Libraries
Women in Medicine
Women in Personnel Management
Women in Printing Trades Group
Women in Publishing
Women in Telecom
The Women's Travel Club of Great Britain

There are many more network groups which may suit your particular profession and it is always worth finding out about their existence through your professional journals, union representative, company newsletters, etc. Not so long ago, after I had given a talk about the problems faced by women managers and how to cope, the firm's Public Relations Officer who had sponsored and organised the workshop came up to me and said:

'I was very interested in what you said in your lecture about using network systems. I have only recently been appointed in this job, and I am the only person doing it as well as the only woman in my office at this management level. I haven't really been trained and no one has told me exactly what my role should be as a Public Relations Officer... They've never had one before, so I don't think management really knows what I should be doing either. I feel very isolated and lost and would love the opportunity of meeting other women doing a similar job to mine.'

Luckily, I happened to know the Chairman of a group known as Women in Public Relations and was able to give this young woman the address, but if you find yourself in a similar situation, then make efforts to find yourself a suitable support network. Another way of doing this is to set up your own woman's group within your organisation, a task which is much easier than you may think. One woman who did just that was Helen Morton, an engineer who helped to set up the Women In BP Group:

'It all began after we had heard the Chairman of the Women In Management Group, who came to give a talk open to all BP employees, and the advantages of forming a company network group was discussed. From the very beginning we had support from Group Personnel and a group of us got together on a regular basis to plan the formation of a Women in BP Group, which eventually formed in 1982. Our general aim is to help women make the best use of their skills and talents, to act as a support network, and to encourage a much greater participation of women in as many areas as possible within the country... The group has an elected organising committee and receives moral and financial support from BP management. As a committee, we have organised numerous public meetings and talks/lectures (men are also encouraged to attend), and have collected statistics and information on development needs of women working in BP. We now publish a yearly report and I am happy to say our membership is growing steadily each month.'

How to start a network

Why not follow Helen's initiative and set up your own company network? Below I've listed guidelines which should help you get your network established:

1. Contact women you know of in your company who would be interested in setting up a network group and arrange an informal meeting at lunchtime or after work. You could also ask the women to invite other women they know to attend.

2. Keep the meeting informal and decide on your aims, how often you would like to meet, whether you wish to include occasional outside speakers, etc.

3. As early as possible involve senior management, e.g. Group Personnel, to get their moral and financial support from the very beginning.

4. It's a good idea to invite someone to come and speak to the group who has started up a women's network in another company in order to give advice and highlight some of the potential problems which can occur. Do this as soon as possible.

5. Advertise the aims of the group, group activities, etc, widely within your organisation. This helps to lower the threat felt particularly by male employees, who may feel that the women are 'ganging up against them'! It will also help to dispel the myth that any women's group is made up of a bunch of 'militant feminist man-haters' – a misconception that can alienate both men and women within an organisation.

6. Adopt the democratic procedures of any official group, e.g. formulate a constitution, elect a chairman, committee members, secretary, and so on. This gives your group status and a certain degree of commitment and security.

7. Try not to alienate certain groups from participating and taking advantage of the group. Often non-professional women such as secretaries feel that the group is not for them, so make sure that a secretarial representative is on the committee and consider inviting outside speakers to tackle issues that may appeal specifically to certain sectors.

8. Consider inviting both men and women to open meetings as this helps to lower the threat from the male quarter. One group, for example, arranged a male versus female debate on the 'nature versus nurture' issue in relation to sex differences!

Making the most of high visibility

'I feel as though a spotlight is always on me and any mistakes I make will be talked about more than those of the men I work with. I feel I must do better than them. If anything, more problems have been encountered by the older men (stick in the muds) who don't seem to realise that women have finally entered their area of work. Some even make sexist comments and I normally take them with a smile and grit my teeth. Others take a more paternal approach. Whatever their approach though, I feel as if I'm always being watched, and closely.'

As a woman manager (especially if there is only one or a few of you) you will be highly visible, which can sometimes lead to a loss of privacy. Having this high profile can mean that any mistakes you make are highlighted. But equally your successes will be highlighted too, and many women are making their visibility work for them rather than against them, as illustrated by this female middle manager:

'I have to admit that when I first started my career the fact that I stood out like a sore thumb, so to speak, did make me a little nervous. Then I began to realise that it wasn't such a bad thing after all. O.K., so the odd mistake was perhaps more obvious than if I'd have been male, but I made sure my successes were noted too and would mention them at the right time and to the right person. The other advantage you have is that most people remember your name (far more than your male colleagues). When one of the managing directors first used to come to the firm for a lunchtime visit I was always introduced to him and very soon he would ask that I sat next to him during meetings and at lunch. I decided to take advantage of this and not only did I let him know my ambitions and what I'd been doing for the organisation but he would often use me as a confidante and tell me policy decisions that not even my boss was aware of. I think that visibility, like anything else which has the potential for working against you, should be approached positively and *used to work for you.*'

Coping with your 'high profile' at conferences and training courses

Being in the minority on training courses and at conferences brings its own problems as regards visibility. In fact, many management trainers are now insisting that their training courses have strong female representation. Ideally of course, a ratio of 50:50 male and female participants would be the figure to aim for but this is not always possible. Interestingly, I have attended a few conferences (usually to do with women at work issues) where there have been just a handful of men, and some of them have complained of feeling the same kinds of visibility pressures that women experience.

Over a drink in the bar after the conference dinner, one male Personnel Officer admitted:

'You know, I've suddenly realised what it must be like for the few professional women who attend courses which are nearly always dominated by men. I, for the first time, feel uneasy being surrounded by so many women. I feel I have to be on my guard as to what I should or shouldn't say, and when I make a comment during the sessions, I realise I'm being listened to very closely!'

I once attended a course which was a week in duration, and out of the 50 people present there were only two of us who were women. While we received and gave needed social support to each other, we were careful not to stick together and become isolated. We shared many common experiences, especially those connected to our high visibility. On one occasion, for example, we both happened to miss attending one of the afternoon lectures. The lecturer stood up at the beginning of the session, gazed into the packed lecture theatre and began with the words: 'Gentlemen, we appear to have lost two ladies overboard!'

Most of us are also aware that conferences away from home can for some be a playground for sexual games, and if you're in the minority you may be a vulnerable target. Rachel is a young scientist and she outlined her coping strategies for these situations:

'When I go to conferences, I am usually the only woman (sometimes initially mistaken for some man's secretary or PA) and within 10 minutes I can now spot the one guy (and there's always one) who is there to have a quick affair. I'm always right and they always make a bee-line for me. I quickly give them the cold shoulder in no uncertain terms. Trouble is, this sometimes makes them even more determined. "Don't tell me your wife doesn't understand you," I say. "Oh no, she understands me but you're so different, so stimulating." They often go away with terrible crushes on me even though I've ignored them, and it's not unusual for me to get phone calls from all over the world from these men long after the conference is over. It's really strange and I think one has to accept that it is often their problem, not yours.'

On the other hand, there are also occasions when people find it easier to handle your high visibility – by pretending you are *invisible*! Joanne related such an experience initiated by a female trainer and how she tackled it:

'I have felt isolated being the lone female on training courses. On a recent course where this was the situation, the course trainer, who was a woman in her early 50s, said

"Come on lads – tea break." Afterwards, I took her aside and had a word with her and said, "I'm also on the course and I happen to be female, not a lad, and I would appreciate being acknowledged." Her reply was "Well, we just don't get females on these courses."

'In fact she did change her style a little. I also had to point out that there were no facilities nearby for ladies toilets as both the toilets were male. I do know that since my complaint one of the toilets has now been converted to female.

'On the whole, I have found that most of the men try their best to make you feel comfortable on training courses. You should try your hardest to fit in, join in, and not feel alien to the group. If all the men go for a swim in the pool before dinner – go with them! You're not aiming to be "one of the lads", just one of the group.'

Consequently, there would appear to be a number of important ways of dealing with the potential problems of being a lone woman on training courses and at conferences, namely:

1. If at all possible make sure that another female colleague (perhaps from another organisation even) also applies to go on the course. If you yourself are responsible for organising or sending people on training courses, try and include a reasonable proportion of women.

2. If there are other women on the course, then offer each other moral support without isolating yourself as a group.

3. Integrate with the men on the course and join in with their activities – you don't have to become 'one of the boys' just part of the team.

4. If you feel you are being discriminated against in any way, then firmly say so and make your feelings known.

5. If you are bothered and pestered by any of the men, then again be firm and confident and use other men with more sympathetic views as allies and support systems.

Dressing for success AND yourself

Whether we like it or not, women in business are judged by their appearance and what they wear, far more than men are. The majority of women managers I interviewed have emphasised the importance of dress. In the words of one senior executive:

> 'Dress is important. I think men have an easier time dressing because if they have a suit then they look respectable, whereas a woman has got to be more careful. If you go to a meeting where there are 12 men and you are the only woman then everyone will look at what you wear, so you have to make sure that you wear something that is acceptable – professional-looking. I do tend to conform in dress as it's easier, and it's a small price to pay in order to gain a little more acceptance. I couldn't afford to be worse dressed than the best dressed secretaries.'

The Americans have taken this issue very seriously and many believe they 'have it licked'. At an international conference on women in management, a well-known American woman in this field exclaimed during her lecture:

> 'I can't understand what all the fuss is about in Europe as regards the professional woman and dress, why not follow the US example? Women managers adopt a smart uniform and there is absolutely no way that she could be mistaken for a secretary.'

Someone from the audience rightly pointed out that the last thing that women managers want to do in Britain is to lose their individuality and conform to male doctrine similar to the now-dying-out breed of bowler-hatted city gents. Becoming more like male managers surely is not the answer, as pointed out by Betty Friedan, who wrote *The Feminine Mystique*, in an interview about American businesswomen:

> 'I had lunch with a group of women executives, and I was horrified. They were so grim, so bitter, so dressed-for-success. And they told me: "We have to be hard-headed, like the men, and get rid of all vestiges of femininity".'

Not surprisingly, learning how to dress is now big business in the US and as Minette Marrin outlined in her article *Honorary Boys*, the result of pseudo male clones is far from pleasing:

'In New York they have clothes consultants to teach women how to dress for success. It seems that American professional women often find the job of sorting out their image, and all its subtle messages of assertion and appeasement, so difficult that they have to hire help.

'Experts will, for huge fees, advise them how to direct attention away from distracting female areas – no ill-placed buttons on the bosom, or front pleats pointing groinwards – and how to avoid colours suggesting vulnerability or threat, and shoes hinting at licentiousness or indecision.

'The results look very depressing. Fifth Avenue is filled with armies of quiet ladies in plain suits of beige and greige, colourless metropolitan mice, understated to the point of camouflage. Their shoes are nearly flat, their make-up is unobtrusive, their hair restrained. For blouses they wear ersatz male shirts and ties, usually something plain with a Mrs Thatcher style tied bow, or (for the more anarchic) a pert little pseudo bow tie. They look like pseudo men.'

The Observer, Nov. 20, 1983, p.1

Although I think we have a lot to learn from the American experience in numerous issues concerning the working woman, this is one case where I believe we should learn from their mistakes. Women managers of today should dress smartly to please themselves and retain their individuality, and not try to adopt the male executive uniform in order to blend in. One can be smart, business-like *and* highly fashionable, and it's up to you to decide on the type of self-image you want to project.

In the final analysis, one must not be coerced into dressing 'up' or 'down' in order to please men. If they cannot accept you as an individual then, as in the case of this male executive, it's *their problem – not yours*:

'Many of my managers and men find it difficult to cope with working alongside women. It could prove a problem if a female wasn't very good-looking or alternatively, was very good-looking – she would need to be in-between on an attractiveness scale. One of the women wore trousers during the day while inspecting the works and tried to be like a man, and at night came out like a butterfly all dressed up and upset the other men posted to that site. They just didn't know how to cope.'

Performance pressure – Do you really have to be better than men?

As already illustrated by a number of previous quotes, professional women, as members of a minority group, often feel that they have to be better than their male colleagues in order to succeed. Moreover, in a survey study of 696 female and 185 male managers and administrators, described in *Stress and the Woman Manager*, *both* the men and the women complained of high stress levels associated with work over-load, time pressures and deadlines, and lack of consultation and communication. However, unlike the men in the sample, women (particularly in middle management positions) complained of high pressure associated with feeling they had to perform *better* at the job than colleagues of the opposite sex. All women managers (including those at supervisory level) were more conscious of making mistakes at work than were men.

This performance pressure is very intense if you find yourself appointed to a particular position in order to act as a test case for the future employment of other women at a similar level. One young female engineer I spoke to complained:

'There is this pressure to prove yourself as you're a woman and breaking ground for future women engineers. You get used to fighting for things such as working on sites, doing your share of night shifts and so on. To a certain extent, I have to be better than my male colleagues. You have got to learn to sell yourself and I think women often have problems doing that.'

Although there are bosses who are guilty of expecting their female employees to perform better than their male co-workers, you should also be aware that this so-called 'performance pressure' can be self-inflicted and there is often a misconception about the issue. As a young female management trainee explained:

> 'Recently I was having a conversation with my male colleagues and they said that they thought that the females would get the better jobs in the company in the long run, and that they don't have to be as good as the men as if they make mistakes – they'll always be given another chance. This totally surprised me, as it was completely opposite to my own opinion – I always feel we have to be better at the job than the men!'

So, you shouldn't feel that you *have* to be better, a pressure one can well do without. There are ways of combating the performance pressure syndrome, namely by learning to sing your own praises, by careful organisation and by skilful time management. A successful senior female executive in the Public Sector gave the following advice on how to conquer performance pressure:

Goal setting
Regarding your work tasks, set yourself targets to reach by certain dates. List them in order of priority.

Organisation
Carefully organise yourself and your work in order to get things done in the time available.

People pressure
Work overload and many pressures are due to the demands made on you by other people. Things will get on top of you if you don't plan your day and work down your list in order of priority. Send a memo to those near the bottom of the list and say it will take a few days or whatever. Apologise in a firm way but don't go home at night worrying about what you've not done.

Delegation
Delegate but don't lose power by delegating.

Resist pressure from above
Don't let your superiors put too much pressure on you, and let them know in a firm way that you are not superhuman and can't be at three meetings at the same time on the same day.

Learn to speak up
If you are asked to do something which is unreasonable, make sure you point out the fact. At the end of the day you will get more respect. Just because you are a woman don't let anyone walk over you or try to get you to take on extra tasks which aren't part of your job – they will most certainly try!

Promotion pays
Remember that dealing with performance pressure gets easier as you climb higher in the organisation; not only does your power increase, but also your experience.

How to enjoy business travel and business entertaining

Most women enjoy business travel, staying in hotels and entertaining clients. However, travelling businesswomen are still the exception rather than the rule and women do report more problems than do men. In most cases though, the problem lies not with the woman but rather with how other people react to her, e.g. hotel staff, waiters and male clients. Businesswomen in the United States and Canada now account for around 30% of the total business travel market – in 1970 the figure was only 1%. In Britain women now constitute about 5% of business travellers, but the number is growing. Congratulations and encouragement are due to Crest Hotels International, who are one of the first hotel chains in Britain to recognise this new market and have carried out an advertising campaign aimed directly at businesswomen. Their double page advertisement in *The Sunday Times* colour supplement led with the phrase: 'I've finally found an hotel that treats me like a man.' They went on to qualify this sensational statement by maintaining that businesswomen who use their hotels are treated like 'people', i.e. they don't have to walk into the bar carrying a briefcase in order to prove that all they want is a drink, or automatically be given a poor table in the restaurant, etc.

There is little doubt that as the numbers increase over the next few years 'this strange travelling creature' will no longer be treated as an oddity and many of the difficulties experienced by women will disappear.

The following vignettes are the personal experiences of three women and they highlight possible pitfalls as well as giving successful ways of dealing with the problems:

Entertaining – 'Waiter, the prices please!'
'As a publicity exec, I often have to entertain clients and journalists in very expensive restaurants, and because it's a male and a female together the waiter would always give me a different menu – the menu *without* the prices! This I found very awkward, especially when my client asked me what I recommended; you can imagine my horror when I had to choose the wine in this situation. I often found myself having to explain very expensive entertainment claims to my company.'

A female saleswoman for a computer firm overcame that situation by using preventative tactics:

'I never have that problem any more as I immediately ask the waiter for another menu – they will know what you mean. If at all possible, I will have a quick word with the waiter as soon as we enter the restaurant (or when booking), letting him know that I am doing the entertaining and that all bills, etc are to be given to me.'

As always, we can rely on the Americans to find a marketable solution to this particular problem, and in the States you can now buy a plastic card costing $6.00, which the female executive can present to the head waiter before her guests sit down. It reads: 'I am a female executive. I am hosting this party. Please instruct service personnel to address all questions to me. When the bill is presented, I am to receive the check.'

The do's and don'ts of business travel and entertaining
'Being an Area Marketing Manager, my work involves me in a lot of travelling about and entertaining clients, and so

over the years I have acquired a number of tips and guidelines which I feel may be useful for other women to follow.'

1. If at all possible, always travel first class.

2. When travelling, always dress smartly. You never know, your client may arrive before you at the hotel and it doesn't look good if you greet him or her wearing your old jeans.

3. On first meeting, clients (who are usually male) may not be used to dealing with a woman on a business level and may be uncertain how to react to you. In fact, if you are with a male colleague you may be mistaken for his secretary or his subordinate and consequently all conversation will be directed towards him and not you. You need to make your position very clear from the start by shaking hands firmly, stating your name and job title. If you then continue in a business-like manner illustrating that you know exactly what you are talking about, from then on you should have few problems. Simply by doing this you put most people at ease.

4. When entertaining, point out to the restaurant staff and your clients that you are the host and will be dealing with the bill.

5. Don't play the token woman – you go to the bar and get the drinks for the men. Even in a social situation with your colleagues in a bar, it is important to pay your way and get in your round. A lot of men don't like you doing this but you should be assertive.

6. One difficult situation when staying in an hotel, is dining out on your own or going to the bar alone. I know many women find this difficult to cope with and feel as if they're there to be picked up. Interestingly, I read recently that in America a woman won substantial damages from a hotel after she was asked to leave the hotel reception area on suspicion of soliciting while she

was a hotel guest. A good idea is to reserve a table as they are then expecting a single female guest for dinner, and you can always miss going to the bar altogether. Alternatively, you can take room service. These tips are only if you aren't happy eating alone. It depends on the hotel atmosphere and if it's a hotel you stay at regularly then you will soon get to know the staff and feel at ease. There are a few hotels/clubs which cater exclusively for women and you may wish to take advantage of those.

7. Finally, *enjoy yourself*. There's nothing nicer than having a relaxing soak in a quiet hotel bathroom with people prepared to wait on *you* for a change, away from the demands of both work and home!

SUMMARY

- If you feel isolated at work, do something positive to alleviate the situation. Form your own social support network with other women in similar positions, e.g. join one of the many professional women's network groups or set up a network group within your own company.

- Do not be afraid to cultivate a mentor/protegée relationship with your boss and take on the responsibility of acting as a mentor for your subordinates, including your secretary.

- Learn to make your visibility work for you and not against you, and do not be afraid of making the odd mistake – it's the successes that count.

- When attending training courses and conferences where you suspect there will be few if any other women attending, try and persuade your employer also to send a female colleague. If you yourself are responsible for organising or sending people on training courses/conferences, make efforts to include a reasonable proportion of women.

- Dress smartly to please yourself and retain your individuality without trying to adopt a pseudo-male 'executive uniform' in order to blend in. You can be smart, business-like *and* highly fashionable.

● Learn to cope with performance pressures; plan and organise your work tasks in order of priority and do not get overloaded or bothered by continual time pressures and deadlines (see also Chapter 6).

● Consider the few basic tips on eliminating potential problems associated with being a travelling businesswoman and with business entertaining – most of all, *enjoy it*!

CHAPTER 5

Becoming Confident and Assertive

'Discouraged from expressing herself forcefully, a girl may acquire speech habits that communicate uncertainty, hesitancy, indecisiveness, and subordination.'

Casey Miller & Kate Swift, *Words and Women*, 1977

It is not surprising that many women managers, particularly at junior and middle management level, maintain that they would benefit greatly in their work and personal life if they gained confidence and acquired assertion skills. From an early age little girls are encouraged to be more dependent and less self-confident than little boys. Judith Whyte in her 1983 report, *Beyond the Wendy House: Sex Role stereotyping in Primary Schools*, revealed that in co-educational primary schools boys got more teacher time and attention than girls, and that the girls' tendency to want to please adults was counter-productive for their future as learners. Instead of becoming curious, restless, adventurous pupils, girls tended to conform and avoid risks and challenges. She concluded that girls should be encouraged to participate in sports and venturesome physical activities in order to help them develop the healthy self-confidence, courage and independence that they later seem to lack.

Obviously, parental influence is very important. For example, all the successful women managers interviewed as case studies for the final chapter in this book emphasised how both their parents (particularly their fathers) had not treated them any differently because they were female. They had been encouraged from an early age to cultivate arguments and opinions of their own, and actively to join in family discussions.

I want to isolate specific situations in which assertive and confident responses will, hopefully, improve your management skills and career prospects. Firstly though, we need to define exactly what is meant by 'becoming an assertive person'.

The assertive person

There is a great deal of misunderstanding about assertion, and particularly about assertion training courses. 'We're not sending women from our firm on one in order to have them become aggressive and bossy' is a comment I got from one Personnel Officer. According to Alberti and Evans in their book *Your Perfect Right: A Guide to Assertive Behaviour*, the assertive person is 'open and flexible, genuinely concerned with the rights of others, yet at the same time able to establish very well his or her own rights.' Consequently, there are fundamental differences between assertive, non-assertive, and aggressive behaviour:

Assertive: You are acknowledging your own rights and those of others.

Non-assertive: You are denying your own right.

Aggressive: You are denying the rights of others.

Being assertive, therefore, is *not* about being bossy, aggressive or selfish. A good example of a situation at work where you may be faced with such a response is one in which you are not being given the recognition you deserve for work done.

Imagine, for example, that you have given a lot of your time and effort to acting as an adviser on an important project with two of your colleagues. They then write up the successfully completed project in the form of a report which will be read by the Managing Director. During a particularly busy afternoon, one of them barges into your office, hands you the typed report and asks you to give it a quick read through *at once* before sending it to the Director. You immediately notice that there are only two contributors' names on the front of the document – and yours is not one of them! What do you say?

Non-assertive response
'Yes of course I will, I'll read it through right now and send it straight back to you.' (You are seething inside and hurt but say nothing and direct your anger inwardly.)

Aggressive response
'Look, can't you see I'm up to my eyes in work? Do you seriously expect me to drop everything just because you decide something requires immediate attention. And why isn't my name on this report? Why should you both get all the credit – just because you wrote it. I'm the one who gave all the expert advice and did all the research. Just who do you think you are!' (You have raised your voice, lost your cool and externalised your anger.)

Assertive response
'I realise that it's important that this is done as soon as possible but I must finish writing this other report in time for a meeting later this afternoon. I'll deal with it as soon as I can and return it to you by 5 o'clock, in time for you to deliver it to the Managing Director's secretary before he leaves the office.

'Ah, I see that my name isn't on the report. I'm sure this is an oversight on your part and I can get my secretary to type on my name before I send the report back to you. I hope that's O.K. with you?' (You have compromised, and made your feelings known in a firm, non-aggressive manner; and *you* should feel 'O.K.')

Sandra Languish, in her chapter on Assertive Training in the book *Improving Interpersonal Relations: Some Approaches to Social Skills Training*, points out the following individual rights which women and men should hope to achieve by being assertive:

- The right to make mistakes.
- The right to set one's own priorities.
- The right for one's own needs to be considered as important as the needs of other people.
- The right to refuse requests without having to feel guilty.
- The right to express oneself as long as one doesn't violate the rights of others.
- The right to judge one's own behaviour, thoughts and emotions, and to take responsibility for the consequences.

Mastering the art of assertion takes time, patience and practice. You will need to do background reading on the topic and useful books include *When I Say No, I Feel Guilty* by Manuel Smith; *Self Assertion for Women* by Pamela Butler; *The Assertive Woman* by Stanlee Phelps and Nancy Austin; *The Cinderella Complex* by Colette Darling; and *A Woman in Your Own Right* by Anne Dickson.

Attending an assertion training course should also prove very beneficial and will enable you to practise your assertion skills in the form of role play, as well as enabling you to get instruction and feedback from an expert trainer and support from the other participants. You will come to realise that you are not alone out there and many people experience exactly the same problems at work as you do.

Sandra Languish adapted the following Assertion Self-assessment Table from Galassi and Galassi, 1977, and has outlined the two-stage approach you need to take to help you identify situations and people with which/whom you have problems in relation to assertiveness, it also enables you to construct your own assertive behaviour hierarchy.

The assertion self-assessment table

Along the left-hand side of the grid there are headings listing the *activities* which represent the major categories of assertiveness: expression of positive feelings, expression of self-affirmation, and expression of negative feelings. The column headings list *people* to whom these activities may be addressed. The people described do not include all the people with whom

Assersion self-assessment table

PEOPLE

ACTIVITY	Friends of the same sex	Friends of the opposite sex	Intimate relations, e.g. spouse, boyfriend, girlfriend	Parents, in-laws, and other family members	Children	Authority figures, e.g. bosses, professors, doctors	Business contacts, e.g. sales-persons, waiters	Co-workers, colleagues, and subordinates
Expressing Positive Feelings Give compliments								
Receive compliments								
Express liking, love, and affection								
Make requests, e.g. ask for favours, help, etc.								
Touch affectionately								
Initiate and maintain conversations								
Self-affirmation Stand up for your legitimate rights								
Refuse requests								
Refuse invitations								
Express personal opinions, including disagreement								
Expressing Negative Feelings Express justified annoyance and displeasure								
Express justified anger								

Source: Adapted by Sandra Languish from Galassi, M.D. and Galassi, J.P., *Assert Yourself*, Human Sciences Press, 1977. I would like to thank Sandra Languish for permission to use some of her material, which she published in Cooper, C.L., *Improving Interpersonal Relations*, Prentice-Hall, 1982

one may interact, and a choice must be made of the individuals who are the most relevant to oneself.

To assess the level of assertiveness in each activity ask yourself 'To what extent do I feel comfortable carrying out this activity with this person?' For example, if you begin with the upper left-hand cell you would form the question, 'Do I feel comfortable giving compliments to friends of the same sex as myself?' If the answer is 'yes', enter a tick in the cell; if the answer is 'no', enter a cross. Continue in this manner for all the cells of the grid. When the table is completed you will be able to identify those people and activities with whom or with which you have difficulty in behaving assertively.

Assertion self-assessment table: evaluation of responses

1. Look at the grid and note where you entered a cross.
   Are there particular *activities* for which you have given a number of crosses?
   List them.

2. Again look at your crosses. Are there any particular *people* to whom you have given a cross?
   List them.

3. Do you behave *aggressively* or *non-assertively*? Shade diagonally those cells in which you behave aggressively, and shade horizontally those in which you behave non-assertively.

4. Identify particular behaviours and people and write: 'I behave aggressively (or non-assertively) when . . . .'

Your own assertive behaviour hierarchy

From the information you have learnt about yourself it is possible to construct an assertive behaviour hierarchy. Select as the first item or situation something you feel you could handle assertively with only minimal anxiety. Continue to order your items from least anxiety-provoking to most anxiety-provoking.

Once you have constructed the hierarchy, it shows up both

long-term and short-term, personally assessed goals which range from the easiest to the most difficult. You may find that the people listed fall into categories such as 'authority figures'; activities may fall into similar groupings, such as 'learning to say no' to unreasonable requests. You will find that during training and through practice, improving behaviour in one setting will probably cause spin-off improvements with related behaviours and people.

Verbal and non-verbal skills

There are two main skills involved in assertion training – verbal skills and non-verbal skills. When being *assertive*, a person generally establishes good eye-contact, stands or sits comfortably without fidgeting, and talks in a strong, steady voice, neither shouting nor mumbling. Assertive talk includes 'I' statements such as 'I think', 'I feel', 'I want', co-operative words such as 'Let's' or 'We could', and empathetic statements of interest such as 'What do you think?', 'How do you feel?'

A non-assertive response is self-effacing and may be accompanied by such mannerisms as the shifting of weight, downcast eyes, a slumped body posture or a hesitant, giggly or whining voice. Non-assertive speech can include qualifiers such as 'maybe', 'I wonder if you could', 'only', 'just', 'would you mind very much', 'I can't', or fillers such as 'you know', 'well', 'uh', and negators such as 'It's not really important', 'It's all right', 'Don't bother'.

An aggressive response is typically expressed by inappropriate anger or hostility which is loudly and explosively expressed. It is characterised by glaring eyes, leaning forward or pointing a finger, and an angry tone of voice. Aggressive words include threats such as 'You'd better', or 'If you don't watch out', putdowns such as 'Come *on*', or 'You must be kidding', and evaluative comments such as 'should', 'I thought you'd know better'.

Indirectly aggressive behaviour uses the language of the non-assertive response combined with the non-verbal behaviour of the aggressive mode, concentrating on body posture and angry movements.

It is important to rehearse and role-play assertiveness in the situations you have isolated, starting with the situations you have listed at the top of your assertion hierarchy list, i.e. the least anxiety-provoking, and work your way gradually down the list. It may take more than one rehearsal and role-play session before a satisfactory level of assertiveness is attained. Don't give up – practise the role-play with a friend, and you can even rehearse on your own looking into a mirror. Once you feel confident about your performance, begin to implement the behaviour in the real world – at work and at home and socially.

You will be surprised by how easily your assertion skills will help you decrease anxious and aggressive feelings and also make you feel more confident and self-assured. On one assertion training course I helped to run for women managers, I recall the words of a 45-year-old Supervisor in the textile industry reporting back to the rest of the group on how her first 'real life' assertive-response turned out:

'For the past year I have been having a really difficult time with one of the secretaries in our main office. She's about my age and whenever I go and see her to get something typed, I usually end up standing by her desk being totally ignored by her while she chats to one of the other secretaries. In the end she'll finally acknowledge me with a grunt. I know that my typing always takes a low priority; one week it took her five days to type a letter for me! She has really been getting me down and it had got to the point where I used to dread going into that office.

'Anyhow, having rehearsed my assertion strategy beforehand, I walked into the office with a letter I needed typing and as usual I got the same reaction – one of total indifference. This time, though, I calmly but firmly asked her if she could come out into the corridor with me for a moment as I wanted to discuss something with her. She looked somewhat surprised but came with me anyway (maybe out of curiosity rather than anything else).

'"For a while now," I said to her, "I've felt there must be

some sort of problem as whenever I come and ask you to do some typing for me you seem unhappy about doing it. Anyhow, I think it's time we sorted it all out so I thought it might be a good idea for us to have lunch together in the pub today."

'She looked at me and mumbled "Yes, O.K." Over lunch we had a good chat and it turned out that she'd never had to work for a woman before and she'd thought that I was "stuck up" and bossy! The change in our working relationship is incredible. If only I'd had the courage to do something about it months earlier I'd have saved myself a lot of unnecessary anguish!'

Applying your assertiveness to specific situations

Meetings – making sure you get your say

From a very early age, little boys are encouraged to be more dominant and aggressive compared to little girls, both in their non-verbal and verbal behaviour.

According to Dale Spender in her book *Man Made Language*, in any group where women are in the minority men will usually talk more than the women and they will interrupt the women more than the women interrupt the men. In other words, men will dominate the conversation. You can test this theory yourself the next time you attend a gathering of any sort, including a luncheon or dinner party.

At work, of course, the most common situation where male domination arises is in meetings. Meetings can often be competitive and, in the business world, men usually outnumber the women present. A common complaint about the frustrations experienced in meetings is described by an up and coming Technical Manager in her late twenties:

'It's always an identical experience for me during meetings. I am the only woman and most of the men are older and more senior than me. They take charge of the meeting from the very start, and before I know it the meeting is over and I've hardly said a word. Often though, I'm bursting inside to make what I think is an important contribution but I either don't get up enough nerve to butt in, or if I do say something, someone interrupts me. I must say I also feel that its only necessary to say something if your contribution is important and relevant – I find men tend to talk just for the sake of talking sometimes. However, I tend to come out of meetings feeling angry at myself and frustrated. I know my boss notices as he has taken me aside twice and told me I ought to say more, but it's not that easy. I feel I've got myself into a rut.'

There are ways of getting yourself out of such a rut and the following sensible tactics were suggested by a senior female executive in the pharmaceutical industry:

1. Prepare notes well in advance of your meeting and make a list of relevant questions or answers to the items on the agenda. Research thoroughly and make sure you've got your facts right.

2. If the majority of participants are men (and particularly if you don't know them very well), make an effort to say something at the start of the meeting. That way, you make it clear you mean business from the very beginning.

3. Don't be afraid to speak up, using a firm, steady voice. If necessary, rehearse points and arguments you wish to raise before the meeting. That way you will feel more confident.

4. If someone interrupts you unnecessarily, then be assertive and do not let them take over, leaving you cut off in mid-sentence. Do not raise your voice, be persistent and if necessary repetitive in your assertive response; e.g. 'Yes Peter, I realise that you disagree with me, but I feel I need to finish what I was saying before you interrupted me. Then by all means, go ahead and make *your* point.'
   It may take some practice – but it does work.

5. Don't go to the other extreme, however, and talk too much (which can sometimes happen if you're feeling nervous).

6. And finally, when it comes to taking the minutes or pouring out the tea, do not take on the secretary or tea-lady role. If the meeting is being held on a regular basis, make it

clear that these tasks should be taken on in turn by everyone present.

Conflict situations – not losing your temper

You can apply assertion skills to all types of work situations, including those which involve conflict. Women are often accused of over-reacting to conflict by being too emotional. One male manager once told me he deliberately avoided any type of conflict with any of his female management trainees, just in case they burst into tears (not that he'd ever seen any of them cry!). On the whole there is no evidence that these assumptions are correct and few people, whether male or female, enjoy conflict situations. Interestingly, in the large-scale survey of women and men managers I carried out with Cary Cooper we found that male managers complained of more pressure associated with the potential conflict situations, such as disciplining subordinates or sacking someone, than did women managers. Certainly, a lot of conflict at work stems from a general lack of consultation and communication – a high stressor we isolated for all levels of female and male managers.

> *Coping with conflict – a female Advertising Executive's account*
> 'When faced with a conflict situation at work, we've all looked back and wished we had reacted differently – "If only I'd said..." I think the best approach is not to over-react. Keep calm, and if you are in a one-to-one conflict, you could well decide you need time to think it over and prepare a rational response. If that's the case, don't be afraid to arrange (in a calm way!) another meeting to discuss the issue more fully. Go away and make notes and think the whole thing out logically. Invite someone else to join the meeting if you are unable to reach a solution. Don't be afraid to compromise, but don't be tempted to give in easily. Never be afraid of asking advice from others either.
> 'If you are in conflict with your boss, it's important to find out what is at the root of it. Often, it may be something completely out of his/her control – an organisational policy change for example.

'A way I cope sometimes is by isolating myself from the workplace. I go out for a walk at lunchtime or say I'm nipping to the bank. That way I can put the whole thing into perspective and create a mini-action plan. Sometimes, I turn on the radio in my car at full blast in order to forget the problem for a while and relax. Nevertheless, the problem won't go away and you have got to tackle it. On some occasions, it's useful to talk to someone who doesn't know a thing about it. Quite often the answer might be very simple. I often talk to a good girlfriend who is in the same line of business.'

Learning to play politics and gain power

An understanding of organisational politics and ways of gaining power is crucial both in terms of being able to get things done by knowing who has the power to help or hinder you, and in assisting in your career development. Managing 'power' enables you to analyse the political framework in which you find yourself. In addition, information is one of the most important political resources, and politically useful information is gained through both formal and informal channels.

Women, especially women in lower management, often complain about feeling unable to manipulate and cope with organisational politics. It is very important for several reasons that women learn to play the political game. Firstly, when a boss has both good human relations skills *and* power, his (or her) subordinates tend to have high morale and loyalty. Secondly, individuals who know how to gain power are likely to become upwardly mobile within the organisation, so it's vital for your career progression. It also follows that promotion is usually accompanied by more personal power. The following exercise entitled The Power Net* will help you clarify your political situation at work. You can draw a

Source: Margaret Ryan and Rennie Fritchie, *Career/Life Planning Workshops for Women Managers*, 1982; Bristol Polytechnic/Manpower Services Commission, p. 53

diagram of your political situation, which may look something like this:

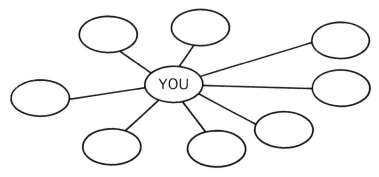

The people round the edge are those who have an important effect on your work. They may be higher or lower than yourself in the hierarchy, and either inside the organisation or outside it (if they are customers for example). Put appropriate names to each of the circles (you can always add extra ones) and then ask yourself the following questions.

- What sort of power does each person in your 'net' have in relation to you?

- Do they have the right to decide what you do, what information you need?

- What is their power based on?

- What sort of power do *you* have in relation to *them*?

You can also think of the power net in terms of dependence. Who depends on you for what? Who do you depend on, for what?

Generally, the activities which will help you to gain power in an organisation are those which:
- Make you visible to the important people within the organisation.
- Are viewed to be somewhat unusual.
- Are seen to be contributing to the solution of an important organisational problem.

Thus, acquiring visibility and admiration for successful actions is an important way of gaining power, and as a woman manager it's highly likely that you have a head start in the visibility stakes anyway!

There are many methods of doing extraordinary things, such as making organisational changes of some kind. Another very important way is by taking risks and succeeding. Women are often less willing to take calculated risks compared to men, and they have a tendency to linger on the negative aspects of risk-taking rather than focusing on the gains.

You should try and analyse how you approach risk-taking and ask yourself the following questions:

1. Do I view risks as a welcome challenge or as something to be avoided at all costs?

2. Do I make a careful calculation before I take a risk and weigh up carefully both the probabilities and the implications of both failure and success?

Successful risk-taking not only heightens your visibility, organisational value and political power, but is obviously an important facet in any manager's work and inherent in problem-solving and decision-making (see Chapter 6). Learning to master the rules of politics at work takes time, so learn from your mistakes and watch and learn from other people. Indeed, I know of many men and women who thrive on political goings-on at work. It's a bit like chess, the more you play then, hopefully, the better you become.

Maintaining your credibility

One can learn a lot about some businessmen's attitudes toward women by listening closely to their conversations. If you become a target for sexist remarks and behaviour, you need to adopt assertive responses in order to deal with the situation satisfactorily and thus maintain your credibility as a professional manager. The following are typical examples of sexist comments:

Scene One: the put-down
You are attending a business luncheon and are the lone woman with four other men. The conversation turns to the complexities involved in providing software for a new home computer.

95

One of the men blasphemes and immediately turns to you and says 'Oh, I'm so sorry, I forgot there was a lady present. By the way, are we boring you?'

Scene Two: the patronised pet
You bump into a male colleague in the local pub. 'Gosh, Rosemary, we blokes were so surprised that you managed to get the client to agree to the Middle East contract – I mean how did you do it? It must be those blue eyes of yours. I said to Mr Jones yesterday, "We're going to have to watch our little girl – she's not just a pretty face." Well done my dear, do let me get you a drink.'

Scene Three: mistaken identity
A hotel guest is dissatisfied with the room he has been given and insists on seeing the manager. When you arrive to discuss his problem, he looks down at you and exclaims, 'But I want to see the manager, not his secretary!'

Scene Four: hitting below the belt
You are attending an important policy meeting and you have been successful in arguing your case for the introduction of a new marketing policy in opposition to a male colleague who is sitting next to you. Realising he is about to be defeated completely, half-way through a sentence he grabs hold of your arm and interrupts with the words, 'Doesn't she look sexy when she gets serious.'

The men described in all these scenes have violated certain communication rules and are engaging in sex role stereotyping which ultimately undermines your position. Patronising, possessive labels such as 'my dear', 'our little girl', and continual reference to your sex should not be tolerated. Men will not put up with being called 'little boys', 'my love', or 'sexy hips!'

Julie, who quickly reached an upper middle management position, has suggested several constructive ways of dealing with these types of sexist remarks:

1. Choose your moment, but soon after you have been subjected to any kind of put-down or sexist remark, let the person know straight away that you don't like it, in a firm, confident and assertive way, e.g. 'I am not "your little girl" John, I am a colleague of yours who happens to be a woman and I feel I must point out that I find it very patronising when you refer to me in that way.' In many cases, the men don't realise what they are saying and its effect.

2. It's much easier to respond assertively with male subordinates and colleagues than it is with your male superiors. However, if you choose the right moment and make your point in a non-aggressive way, you may be pleasantly surprised by his reaction. I recall one of my previous bosses coming into my office first thing one morning and saying, 'You know, after what you said yesterday, I went home and said to my wife "Do you find it patronising when someone calls you 'my dear'?" She replied that she did. I was astounded, as I've been calling women that all this time and I thought I was being friendly, not offensive!'

3. Another tactic to use is along the lines, 'You're not prejudiced against women at work are you?' Even though they *may well be*, very few men will openly admit it to you. By making such a comment, they then become far more aware of any prejudices they may have towards you. It makes them *think* and often helps you as they think, 'I can't get away with it with this one!'

4. Always point out to the offending person that your career is just as important to you as theirs is to them and that you wish to be treated as another individual, who is a manager and just happens to be a woman.

5. If you lack confidence, practise and rehearse responses to sexist comments either with a friend or at home looking at yourself in a mirror. It's definitely worth the effort involved – you gain the respect you deserve and maintain your credibility.

Therefore, never accept the stereotyped roles that people at work might try and force upon you, whether it be the pet, the sex object, the mother-earth confessor, or the feminist man-hater. These roles undermine a woman's self-image and undervalue her competence. The concept of androgyny, i.e. the combination of both male and female qualities, such as emotional expressiveness and decisiveness, was originally devised by Bem and is a trait which has been shown to be most beneficial for women subjected to role imposition. According to Bem '... the androgynous individual is someone who is *both* independent and tender, *both* aggressive and gentle, *both* assertive and yielding, *both* masculine and feminine, depending on the situational appropriateness of these various behaviours.'

There is no doubt that it is not always easy to resist role alignment but the rewards of doing so are worthwhile. The following optimistic attitude towards the roles adopted by some women at work came from a top female executive:

'There seem to be three types of career women stereotypes in industry: The "army tweed and brogues" type, the "burning bra" type and the "easy floozy" type. The answer I have developed over a time is to ensure that managers get to know me as a person. I deliberately disclose aspects of myself and my life which defy stereotypes. I also refuse to be "miracle woman" and I let the men know when I'm not coping.

'I have experienced an identity crisis at work. There are expectations and temptations to be like men, the "one of the lads" syndrome. How feminine should I be in dress, behaviour and general appearance? The release of tension when I decided to be "me" was enormous. I'm my own personality and *that* I will *not* trade for my career.'

SUMMARY

● Mastering the art of assertion takes time, patience and practice. You will need to do background reading and if possible attend an assertion training course.

● It is essential to rehearse and role-play the situations you isolate as requiring assertive responses, starting with the least anxiety-provoking and threatening ones. Once you feel confident about your performance, begin to transfer that behaviour to the real world.

- Make sure you apply your assertiveness skills in meetings and get your say.

- Learn to handle conflict situations without losing your temper.

- Remember, politics is about power. Try to understand organisational politics and use it to assist your career development.

- Do not allow yourself to become a target for sexist remarks or sex role stereotyping. Practise assertive responses in order to deal with such situations satisfactorily and thus maintain your professional credibility.

- Apply your assertion skills when it comes to becoming an effective manager and adopt an androgynous style of management.

CHAPTER 6

Dealing with Stressful Situations and Prejudice

'Women ought to understand that in submitting themselves to this swindle of underpayment, they are not only insulting themselves, but doing a deadly injury to the community.'

Rebecca West, *The Young Rebecca: Selected Essays by Rebecca West, 1911–1917*, edited by Jane Marcus, 1982

If you are a working professional woman it is very important that you know to what extent the stresses and strains of your position may affect your physical and mental health and overall well-being.

What is meant by the word stress? Well, to begin with, life is stress – in fact, without a certain amount of stimulation we become bored and consequently stressed! We are all different and each one of us needs a certain level of stimulation – for some of us (the 'stress seeker' types), that level is quite high; for others it is much lower. We say that someone is 'under stress' when the pressures are such that the individual is no longer able to cope.

The annual cost to the nation due to absenteeism from work as a result of stress-related illness has recently been estimated to be £3,000 million per annum, or £132 per employee. On top of this there are hidden costs such as the reduction in performance of employees who are suffering from anxiety, depression or even a straightforward headache brought on by acute work pressure or tension. Research indicates that professional women tend to have higher self-esteem and better mental health than homemakers of similar educational status, but, in comparison, they lack relaxation time. For some (especially if you are a working wife and mother), the excessive pressure and scarcity of free time can adversely affect stress-coping abilities and result in illness and behavioural problems.

I have already discussed many of the specific problems and pressures associated with being a female manager and professional, e.g. burdens of coping with the role of the 'token woman', lack of role models, feelings of isolation and the strains of coping with sex stereotyping. In the study I carried out with Cary Cooper we discovered that besides the extra stresses experienced by women managers associated with trying to maintain a family and/or home (to be discussed more fully in Chapter 7), the higher work-related pressures reported by women were often in some way associated with prejudice and sexual discrimination. Therefore, the emphasis of this chapter will be on how to isolate your own pressure sources at work and on ways of coping with them successfully, particularly with stressors linked to discrimination.

Isolating your own pressure sources at work

Stress can manifest itself in a number of ways including physical and mental ill health and behavioural symptoms, for example:

Stress outcomes

Physical ill health	*Mental ill health*
Heart disease and heart trouble	Depression
Hypertension	Anxiety
Asthma	Phobias
Hayfever	Sleep problems
Repeated skin trouble	Loss of appetite
	Tiredness

Stress outcomes continued

Physical ill health	*Mental ill health*
Ulcer (stomach)	Shortness of breath
Trouble with gastro-	Trembling
intestinal tract	Irritability
Cold or flu	Etc
Migraine or severe headaches	
Etc	

Behavioural outcomes	
Cigarette smoking	Job dissatisfaction
Alcohol and drug abuse	Poor job performance
Home problems, e.g. marital	Accidents
disharmony	Suicide
Divorce	Etc

In his book *The Stress Check*, Cary Cooper identifies early behavioural symptoms which will enable you to recognise stress in yourself and others. These include:

- Difficulty in thinking rationally and seeing all aspects of a problem.
- Rigidity of views, prejudice.
- Out-of-place aggression and irritability.
- Withdrawal from relationships.
- Excessive smoking.
- An inability to relax resulting in excessive drinking or a need for sleeping pills.

If you can identify with any of these symptoms, then it is highly likely that certain people and/or situations are causing you stress, and you should try and identify your own pressure sources at work. (You can also be thinking about home pressures as we shall be dealing with these in more depth in the next chapter.)

I should emphasise that the findings in the Davidson and Cooper study *did not* suggest that women in managerial positions cannot cope with stress. What we suggested was that females in managerial positions are often faced with *additional pressures* both from work and home/social environment not experienced by male managers. Hence, it is important that as a

Table 6.1 *Higher reported pressure levels at work by 696 female managers (compared to 185 male managers)*

Factors intrinsic to the job
- Business travel and staying in hotels alone.

The token woman
- Lack of same sex role models.
- Sex stereotyping role imposition.
- Performance pressure.

Career development
- Sex a disadvantage re job promotion/career prospects.
- Sex discrimination and prejudice.
- Inadequate job training experience compared to colleagues of opposite sex.
- Colleagues of opposite sex treated more favourably by management.

Relationships at work
- Members of opposite sex seem uncomfortable working with women because of their sex.
- Experiencing prejudiced attitudes at work because of their sex from members of the same sex and opposite sex.
- Feeling uncomfortable on training courses when a member of the minority sex.
- Sexual harassment.
- Lack of encouragement from superiors.
- Lack of social support from people at work.

Source: Davidson and Cooper, *Stress and the Woman Manager*, Martin Robertson, 1983

woman in management you are aware of potential pressure points, that you isolate them and do something constructive to alleviate them.

Exercises for isolating pressure sources

These next two exercises will help you to pinpoint your own pressure soures:

1. Defining *pressure* as a problem, something you find difficult to cope with and about which you feel worried or anxious, list your own major pressure sources *at work*.

2. Maintain your own *stress log* (see Figure 6.2). This should provide you with information about the type of event or person or situation that causes you the most difficulty. An awareness of this should help you to develop an action plan to minimise or eliminate the stressor, or at the very least make you aware of when a stressful event (in your terms) is about to take place.

Figure 6.2 *Stress log/diary*

Stress can come from a single dramatic incident, or from a cumulation of less dramatic incidents. At the end of each working day next week describe:

1. The most stressful single incident that occurred on your job (confronting a staff member, etc).

2. The most stressful series of related incidents that occurred on your job (frequent telephone interruptions, etc).

	Single incident	*Series of related incidents*
Monday		
Tuesday		
Wednesday		
Thursday		
Friday		

Please indicate below other stressful incidents which usually occur but did not this week:

Source: Copyright held by Walter H. Gmelch and Boyd Swent from material published in *Stress at the Desk and How to Cope Creatively*, Oregon School Study Council, 1977

How to cope with stress

Having talked about what is meant by the term 'stress' and looked at some exercises which will help you isolate and consider some of the stressors in your work life, I now want to turn your attention to the important issue of how you learn to cope with your stress.

Make yourself an action plan

If you have a pretty good idea what the major stressors in your life are, then in most cases there are usually *constructive* ways of dealing with these pressure sources. You will need to make the effort to set yourself an action plan in order to minimise stress.

List the stressors you have isolated in the previous two exercises, and then write down the non-constructive strategies and behaviours which you may be using in response to each stressor. Next, list the constructive coping strategies which would help you eliminate each problem and its associated pressures. For example, if one of your stressors is work overload, you may come up with the following:

Stressors

Work overload: Having too much to do and too little time to do it (resulting in tiredness, poor work performance).

Non-constructive responses	*Coping strategies*
Taking on more work; not saying no to extra work (i.e. being non-assertive).	Delegating. Learning to say no and being assertive.
Poor time management.	Becoming more organised.
Setting myself impossible deadlines.	Not setting impossible deadlines.

Coping with hurry sickness

A certain type of behaviour, referred to as coronary-prone 'Type A' behaviour or 'hurry sickness', has been associated

105

with the onset of stress-related illness, particularly heart disease, and with behavioural reactions such as smoking. Although coronary heart disease and lung cancer have been predominantly 'male' diseases in the past, there are indications both in the USA and Britain that death from these two major causes is on the increase in women entering the workforce and consequently being exposed to occupational stress. Moreover, much of the research investigating Type A behaviour in the work setting suggests that stress within the work environment itself enhances Type A behaviour patterns.

Bearing in mind these findings, and the fact that women managers tend to have higher Type A scores than their male counterparts, now is the time to assess your own degree of hurry sickness and take action to control it.

Type A behaviour is characterised by a style of living which includes the following:

- Extremes of competitiveness.
- Striving for achievement.
- Aggressiveness.
- Haste.
- Impatience.
- Restlessness.
- Hyper-alertness.
- Explosiveness of speech.
- Feelings of being under pressure of time and under the challenge of responsibility.
- Inability to relax without feeling guilty.
- Few outside non-work interests.
- A form of angry hostility towards others; a belief that you can't depend on people being nice to you, that most of them are going to be mean to you.

If you can identify with most of these characteristics, it's very likely that you are a Type A – and the more Type A you are, the higher your chances of eventually developing a stress-related illness. But do not despair as there are various techniques and methods you can follow to manage your hurry sickness, such as:

- Force yourself to listen to other people.
- Talk only when you need to.

- Try to control your obsessional time-directed life.
- Allow reflective periods to assess the causes of your hurry sickness. Understand that the majority of your work and social life does not really require immediate action.
- Broaden yourself by indulging in outside activities – cinema, theatre, reading, sport, etc.
- Try not to make unnecessary appointments and give yourself unachievable deadlines.
- Protect your time, learn to say no.
- Take as many stress-free breathing spaces during the course of an intensive work day as possible.
- Try to create opportunities during the day or night when you can relax entirely your body and mind.

Exercise, diet and relaxation

Other ways of relieving the stress in your life include making sure you eat properly and healthily, getting yourself physically fit, and practising relaxation techniques. It is worth remembering that stress exhausts energy, and physical exercise is energising and can also give you a 'high' – a feeling of well-being. The main thing is to find a form of exercise which you enjoy (personally, I've yet to see a jogger with a happy, smiling face!). Exercise can also help you keep your weight in check when combined with a well-balanced diet which is low in salt, animal fats and sugar.

Secondly, discover what type of activity makes you feel most relaxed. For some it may be listening to music, for others it may be relaxation exercises. (And don't be afraid to discover new ways of relaxation such as self-hypnosis, yoga or meditation.) Set yourself a strict routine of at least 15 minutes a day (you could break these up into five-minute periods) in which to carry out your relaxation routine. These periods should be times when you are on your own completely undisturbed. One personnel officer told me that the only way she could escape from her family each evening to relax was by locking the bathroom door and soaking in the bath. I also know some executives who take five-minute breaks at work by closing their office doors and getting their secretaries to answer all calls. The benefits are well worth it.

Seeking support

Next, don't be afraid to seek social support from other people and talk about your problems. (Men in particular tend not to do this and consequently internalise their worries which results in tension, frustration and depression.) In some cases you may need to seek professional, confidential advice from, for example, Personnel, Marriage Guidance, Alcoholics Anonymous, etc.

You can find out more about identifying stress sources and ways of coping successfully with stress by further background reading (see the suggested reading list). Given the opportunity, you should also try and attend a Stress Reduction and Awareness Workshop.

Whatever coping strategies you decide to pursue, the important rule to remember is never to neglect a problem and hope it will go away. *Do something constructive now.*

Who copes best?

How come some people seem to cope with stress better than others? We all know of friends and colleagues who appear to cope even when they experience very traumatic and stressful events, while others seem to crack under the strain very quickly.

An American psychologist, Dr Suzanne Kobasa, has found that people who undergo great stress yet stay healthy share certain characteristics. They include having a sense of purpose, feeling in control of your life, and viewing unexpected events as challenges rather than threats. She calls these stress-resistant people 'hardy', and a feeling of control enables them to redirect stressful situations to their advantage. To get a sense of your own control over your stress, consider how you would handle a frustrating situation such as missing a train. If you take advantage of the time by reading the paper or doing some work, you are in control of your stress. If you spend the time feeling anxious and angry about what made you late or about the meeting you've missed, your stress is controlling you.

What you must try and do, is feel in control of the pressures in your life. Try to take a more positive approach, and when faced with stressful situations think positive thoughts such as: 'I can handle this'; 'This is not threatening'.

Decision-making under pressure

As stress can affect your preformance at work, it may be useful for you to practise your decision-making skills under pressure by completing the following exercise. Not only does this exercise show up your coping skills when under pressure, it also incorporates other skills which I have already covered, such as time management, being assertive, and politics and power issues.

Your priority assignment

Problem

You (the manager) left on Monday for a one-week company-sponsored training programme in leadership. Your department was handed over to Ms R, but she became ill and went home. It was then handed over to Ms K, but her mother became critically ill and she went home. You were telephoned two hours ago and asked to return on an emergency basis. You arrived five minutes ago. The time is 1.00 p.m. The day is Friday. When you walk into your office you face 10 critical problems.

Procedure

These problems are listed below. Please read, evaluate, and give a priority number to each problem. In other words, decide which problem you should handle first, second, third, and so on.

A ( ) You have received a report from Ms Personnel that Ms L is looking for another job outside the company. She wants you to talk to her. You reckon that this would take you 15 minutes.

B ( ) Mr Big has left word that he wants to see you in his office immediately upon your return. Anticipated time: 60 minutes.

C ( ) You have some very important-looking unopened mail (both company and personal) on your desk. Time: 10 minutes.

D ( ) Your telephone is ringing.

E ( ) A piece of equipment has broken down, halting all production in your department. You are the only one who can fix it. Anticipated time: 30 minutes.

F ( ) A very attractive man is seated outside your office waiting to see you. Time: 10 minutes.

G ( ) You have an urgent written notice in front of you to call a Birmingham operator. Both your mother and the company headquarters are located in Birmingham. Time: 10 minutes.

H ( ) Mr Demanding has sent word he wants to see you and has asked that you return his call as soon as possible.

I ( ) Ms Q is in the staff lounge and says she's ill. She wants your permission to go home. It will take about 15 minutes to get the facts and make a decision.

J ( ) In order to get to your office by 1.00 p.m., you had to miss lunch. You are very hungry, but you estimate it will take 30 minutes to get something substantial to eat.

Desirable rank-ordering
The following rank-ordering is considered to be in a woman manager's best interests:

B 1 Mr Big is the Chairman. He also has a much bigger picture of the company. Just as important, you don't want to miss any opportunity to gain access to the top.

E 2 Get production moving.

G 3 High priority. Either way, headquarters or mother, you'll work better if anxiety is eased.

A 4 This is high because Ms L may be a key employee and the discussion will only take 15 minutes.

C 5 It's waited all week; it can wait a few more hours.

I 6 If Ms Q were really sick she'd have gone home. It may seem inhumane, but this is not high priority.

D 7 Low priority. Let your secretary answer and filter your calls.

H 8 Low priority. He's probably an everyday nuisance.

F 9 Usually game-players decide to put this and J (lunch) together.

J 10 Either send out for a sandwich and eat it while you do E and G, or wait and go with F.

Source: This exercise was slightly adapted by Margaret Ryan and Rennie Fritchie in *Career/Life Planning Workshops for Women Managers*, Bristol Polytechnic/Manpower Services Commission, 1982, from Cannie J.E., *The Woman's Guide to Managerial Success*, 1979, and is reproduced by permission of Prentice-Hall Inc, Hemel Hempstead

Coping with prejudice and discrimination from men

Men who are most likely to hold prejudiced views about women as managers and professionals are either those members of the 'old school' who hold traditional views about women's place in society and normally have non-working wives, or younger men who feel highly threatened by the 'infiltration' of very competent, professional women:

The threatened male – an extremist view
'Let's face it. Most women don't want careers, they don't want to be the same as men. I think there's something very odd about a woman who wants to be a manager in our industry, it's odd to choose a masculine career. Mind you, I don't think men should go into nursing either. Men promote men on the whole and that's how it should be. It's unfair on other men if women are treated any differently or if women are promoted because they're women – this also causes resentment. I think you shouldn't recruit women in the first place. They are a minority and should be kept out – too many men resent having women in this structure. They

are seen as career blocks and as being candidates for preferential treatment.

'However, don't get me wrong. I don't dislike all women who work, they are perfectly O.K. as long as they stick to traditionally female careers.'

The best way to deal with prejudiced attitudes like the above when they are directed towards you is to confront the individual in an assertive way and let your opinions be known. Ginny, a young trainee manager, works in a traditionally male environment and has worked out ways of dealing with threatened male colleagues:

'I've been working with a man who isn't as highly qualified as me but has more management experience. He feels threatened by me and can be aggressive. I've had other male colleagues tell me they don't think as a married woman, I should be working. It often makes me feel cross inside but I still think it's important that you put forward your own point of view without getting angry. If you don't say anything in response, then they'll continue to make such prejudiced comments. By saying something you can some-times make them stop and think. I never let it get me down though, and use other female and sympathetic male col-leagues in order to get support.'

One has to acknowledge that changing ingrained attitudes is not an easy task. On the brighter side, however, the new generation of younger male managers have far more enlight-ened attitudes towards women in professional and leadership positions, and these positive attitudes appear to be enhanced as more and more women enter the previously male domains.

A recent survey of male executives in a multinational's subsidiaries in England, Holland, Belgium, France and Ger-many revealed that lack of personal experience of working with women senior executives was an important reason underlying men's resistance to women's entry as heads of subsidiaries. Those men who believed that a well-qualified woman could not head a subsidiary also said they knew of none. However, the men who had either met or worked with women subsidiary heads were more receptive to the possibility.

Nevertheless, one has to accept that there may be situations where (due to organisational and/or superiors' prejudicial attitudes) your management career progression prospects may be very poor. If this is the case, my advice is to look for another job in a more 'enlightened' company.

Men have problems too!

To some extent the difficulties between men and women attempting to work together as equals in harmony have tended to be concentrated on the problems faced by women. Nevertheless, we should remember that men can also be 'victims' of their conditioning and many have great difficulty in knowing how to react to women as colleagues and/or superiors. Encouragingly, more and more management trainers are acknowledging this fact, and mixed gender courses are emerging which are concerned with the issue of men and women working successfully together.

A young male engineer I interviewed gave the following honest confession about his own personal problems involved in coming to terms with working alongside female engineers:

'It is essential that people realise that it takes time and effort by men to accept women as engineers. The first time you see someone from outerspace, you don't know how to react – prejudice is bound to be there because it's strange. It takes time to adjust. I know I found it strange when I first worked with a woman engineer. I felt odd, and didn't know how to react. Now, I'll know how to relate to other female engineers, but it took me months to get the working relationship going and I think that's typical of what goes on for other men.

'I really think this issue should be investigated and understood more and there should be training workshops to deal with it. In my case, I had problems: this woman wasn't a sister, wife or secretary and I felt strange. With secretaries, it's different as you know where you are; there's a certain distance and respect. With women engineers, though, it's a completely different experience altogether.'

Men working for women

I once asked a number of branch managers in a large multinational how they would feel working for a woman. A few confessed that they would definitely not like it, but for the majority, the thought was totally alien to them and they had no idea how they would react. What I have found is that senior male executives are often over-sensitive and over-cautious about the way in which they think male subordinates are going to react to a female boss. For example, Frank (a young Housing Officer) has a woman boss and asserted that for him it had more advantages than disadvantages:

> 'I never really thought about having a woman as Head of Section when I was appointed to this job. In fact, I much prefer it, I get on very well with her and compared to my other bosses, who have all been men, she is much more co-operative and far more people-orientated in her management style.'

Obviously there are some men (and women) who don't like working for women and I have interviewed a few women managers who have said that male employees have asked to be transferred because a woman had been appointed above them. However, these are the exceptions rather than the rule. One single female entrepreneur, with her own successful business, admitted that she deliberately employed married men to work for her as they were more stable and less of a threat. She went on to say:

> 'I think women have to be more diplomatic in leadership positions. Men can dictate orders, whereas if women do that they are classed as having a personality problem.'

There are also cases where men working for women try and use their sex to get on, as described by Penny, an area manager:

> 'I have found that in counselling or interview situations, men become extremely shy and nervous because I'm a woman and their boss, and I have to go out of my way to put them at ease. However, there are men who try to get round you by using their "sexual charms" to get on – running

around getting you tea (when you don't really need it!), or rushing to get you a chair. You have to be quite blunt occasionally when the fawning gets too much and basically let them know that that's *not* the way to get on!'

Sexual harassment

Sexual harassment is another potentially stressful situation linked with prejudicial male attitudes and behaviour. Raise the subject of sexual harassment at work to men and often the reaction is one of humour, and comments such 'I should be so lucky – where do I go to get sexually harassed?' abound! Clearly, they have misunderstood the definition of the term. Sexual harassment can be defined as *unwelcomed* sexual advances, requests for sexual favours and other verbal, or physical, conduct of a sexual nature. Consequently, the emphasis is on the word *unwelcomed* – flirtatious or sexual behaviour between consenting adults is not sexual harassment. Interestingly, the few men I know who have been victims of sexual harassment by women at work (in many cases a female secretary or student) have found it incredibly difficult to cope with. Women, on the other hand, have often been subjected to harassment of some kind or other since their early teenage days when they were wolf-whistled and jeered at by workmen.

A 1982 survey by the National Council for Civil Liberties found that more than one in ten working women in Britain had felt that a man had been taking advantage of his position at work to make persistent sexual advances towards them. Divorced and separated women seemed to be particularly vulnerable. Over a quarter of the sample admitted that they had been the victims of this kind of sexual harassment.

Women in professional and management positions are in no way immune from sexual harassment. The incidence of sexual harassment experienced by the 60 women manager interviewees in *High Pressure* was disturbing, with 52% of the sample saying they had experienced sexual harassment at work. Women occupying middle and junior level management positions, were more likely to have been victims than were senior female executives. Young women sexually harassed by a male superior are in a particularly distressing situation. A woman in her twenties in marketing told me of such an experience and how, in hindsight, she should have tackled it:

'In one of the departments I used to work in, I had a boss (section leader) who made me physically ill by his continual sexual harassment. I was afraid to come into work and being called into his office. He'd close the door and start grabbing me and making sexual remarks. It got so bad that I was ready to quit, but luckily my manager promoted me, so I left that department.

'I never did complain, but eventually two or three girls who went into that section after I'd left got together and complained to Personnel about this same man. Personnel then called me in to ask if I'd had similar trouble, so I told them everything that had happened. The man is still a section leader and has been promoted to a higher grade, but he has no women working for him – which is deliberate of course.

'At the time I didn't do anything about it as I didn't want to get him sacked. I think, though, in reality I knew they wouldn't do anything except give him a warning. Anyway, it would have been my word against his and who'd have believed me?

'I think I'd cope with it better now as I'm older. I would try and nip it in the bud before it developed. It got out of hand very quickly. I would also have gone to Personnel if it had continued. At the time, my husband threatened to come to work and beat the bloke up, but I realised it wouldn't have solved the problem.'

Another senior female administrator relayed her techniques for nipping flirtatious remarks in the bud:

'Some men have only ever had experience of knowing women as secretaries or wives and don't know how to cope when working with a professional woman. They often flirt with you and it takes a few years to learn how to cope with it. I am consistent myself and stop listening to or accepting flirtatious remarks. If someone flirts or puts you down sexually, the best way is to confront them. They often don't realise they're doing it and stop if you point it out to them.'

116

How to combat sexual harassment

In America, sexual harassment is now treated · seriously, having become an economic issue whereby punitive damages have been awarded against companies for sanctioning the behaviour of harassers. Conversely, to quote the NALGO leaflet, *Sexual Harassment is a Trade Union Issue*, 'In Britain awards by tribunals for sexual harassment (it crops up most often in cases of "constructive dismissal", i.e. where a woman has been forced to leave her job because of sexual harassment) are derisory, and it had been difficult to get employers or the media to treat the issue with any seriousness.'

However, sexual harassment is now becoming a trade union issue in this country. The Trades Union Council have issued a booklet with guidelines on how to deal with 'it', as have NALGO, Britain's largest white collar union. Other smaller unions are following suit, as illustrated by this newspaper extract entitled 'Pinned Down':

'A Fleet Street woman engineer (one of a tiny number) complained about pin-ups. The manager turned nasty and her fellow workers supported him. The union stepped in, and some of the pin-ups have now been removed. A more important result was the formation of the union-based London Print Campaign against Sexual Harassment which is providing a support network and practical help. Meetings are regular (non union members would be welcomed) and there's a free leaflet.'

The Guardian, Nov. 23, 1983, p. 10

But, if you are not in a position to get support and advice from your union, union representative or Personnel, there are ways of dealing with sexual harassment. In her book *Sexual Harassment at Work*, Sue Read proposed a number of procedures to follow which are summarised below:

1. Be aware when the stream of personal remarks begins, the 'accidental' bumping into and touching, the ways in which he tries to be alone with you. Sexual harassment can be stopped before it becomes a pattern.

117

2. At the first sign of a male co-worker or boss doing or saying anything which makes you feel uncomfortable, don't ignore it. Make it clear to him how you feel about it. There is no need to do this publicly to begin with, find a private way of telling him that you don't like that sort of behaviour, that it makes you feel uncomfortable. Tell him that you want to continue to work together as friends, and suggest that he does not do it again.

3. If the harassment still continues, start keeping a diary of events, including dates of when and where harassment takes place.

4. Talk to other women who work in the same place about it and ask them if they have ever had experience of unwanted sexual attention. Explain to them what is happening to you. Many harassers will have tried other female workers, and it is their experiences that you need – not only to prove your case, but also to help you realise that you aren't alone, you aren't to blame, and this isn't an isolated incident which you alone can't handle.

5. When you go and ask the person who is harassing you if he will stop, take a work colleague with you, both for your confidence and so that you have a witness present in case at a later stage he denies that you ever asked him not to do it. Having a third person there proves that you're serious enough to have told someone else, and this could embarrass him so much it will stop him.

6. If all this fails and the harassment continues or gets worse, write him a polite letter explaining from your point of view what you think is happening, giving exact dates and places for everything that has taken place, however small. You have to make it clear to him that you are taking all this very seriously and have been keeping an account of events.

    Then describe how his actions make you feel – whether it is disgust, misery, revulsion or only embarrassment and worry. The letter should end by saying what you would like to see happen. You may just want the harassment to stop. If so, then say so. If possible, you should deliver this letter in person (taking another person with you as a witness), so that you know it has arrived. Keep a copy of it for yourself, in case you should need to refer to it.

It has been found that, when a letter has been written, the harasser generally says nothing but reforms his behaviour. Sometimes there is an apology or a denial, and at other times even a discussion about it. Hardly ever is there a reply in writing, but nevertheless the alleged harassment usually stops, especially in the case of mild harassment, such as innuendo or sexual suggestion.

7. Finally, it is most important not to be frightened or feel stupid, and above all don't feel guilty. All you are doing is explaining to another person how you feel about something they are doing to you. Forget about guilt or blame, and don't feel that you are behaving like a prude or a spoilsport.

Dealing with prejudice and discrimination from women

The female boss – dragon or mentor

As we have all heard before, women can turn out to be their own worst enemies, and women don't always enjoy working with, or for, other women. The 'queen bee' label for a certain type of female boss is perhaps the best known when it used to describe a woman in a position of power who feels that she had to work hard and make sacrifices, so why should she make it easier for others? She also tends to be unhelpful to other women, partly because of her desire to remain unique in the organisation and partly because she is fearful of the competition. However, in my experience, the new executive woman is not a member of the 'old school dragons' and is usually very concerned about helping other women, as well as adopting a mentor role (see Chapter 4).

Do you have to 'woo' female subordinates and secretaries?

Undoubtedly women in leadership and managerial positions do sometimes complain of prejudice, resentment and lack of co-operation from women who work for them. The problem tends to be most common with younger female managers who have secretaries and older women working for them who are unused to having a woman as a boss. Louise found herself in that situation after her recent promotion to a senior position in the company at the age of 28, and she described to me how she dealt with the problem which emerged:

Female clerks
'Coping with prejudiced attitudes towards you from women is very different to prejudice from men – in many ways it's as hard, if not harder. After my recent promotion at work, the senior clerk who deals with handing out my wage slip said as she handed it to me: "There you are dear – that'll help with the household budget and be a bit of pin money for you." (I'd recently got married and her inference was that as a woman I shouldn't be earning that much money.) She was the sort of woman who needed dealing with by just laughing and taking the cheque. By laughing, I showed my confidence; by going overboard in my reaction, I would have been inviting her to do it a lot more often.'

Secretaries
'With female secretaries, I do feel in some ways that because you are a woman you have to woo them at first, whereas men don't feel they have to do this. I do think you have to ascertain that you are assertive, confident and a manager in your own right. There are small things you need to watch out for as far as some secretaries are concerned. For example, I have found, especially with middle-aged female secretaries, that they often find it very difficult to accept that you *don't* want them to put Miss or Mrs at the end of your memos or letters. They're happy to accept Christian name initials and surnames for men but want to classify your marital status if you're a woman.'

Other female subordinates
'All in all, I've found that most difficulties have stemmed from middle-aged women at middle supervisory level, who initially didn't want to accept my authority because I was a young female – many of them gave the impression they were jealous. This was a difficult one to cope with and for a long

time I tried to become friends with them in order to affect my authority. This friendship was achieved via discussions about their interests outside work, such as holidays, etc, before actually approaching work subjects. Then the approach I used was to show my genuine interest in them by offering help and advice if they wanted to get on by going on training courses, etc. Many didn't want to, but some did. The result is, that they all respected my encouragement and what I wanted to do in the organisation, plus my expertise and authority. I don't have any difficulties now.'

Introducing positive action

Looking on the optimistic side, more and more organisations are taking the initiative and implementing their own positive action projects, e.g. Thames Television, National Westminster Bank, West Midlands Bank, the University of Aston, and BP (UK). Positive action programmes provide for equal opportunity by the elimination of bias in employment practices and by giving special encouragement to women (and men) moving into non-traditional jobs. A number of companies now employ an Equal Opportunities Manager to carry out positive action, which will evaluate and reassess career opportunities, devise new career structures to enable movement into formerly unavailable positions and occupations, ensure special training, including on-the-job training denied in the past, and build up equal opportunity awareness and skills training for supervisors, managers, and interviewers.

Since the appointment of a Women's Employment Officer at Thames Television a lot has changed. Management training on how to avoid sex discrimination has started, and they have produced a new booklet on non-discriminatory codes of practice for interviewing. Financial assistance for child day care is now offered to male and female employees, and company crèche places are being provided. There are also improved company benefits for maternity leave. Company profiles are produced regularly to detail the position of women and their progress through the organisation, and Television Training Courses are open to all staff to attend and learn the mechanics of television programme-making, as well as to take advantage of career counselling.

Working out your own positive action programme

You can always take the initiative yourself with the support of female colleagues and work out your own positive action programme. Sadie Robarts, A. Coote and Elizabeth Ball, in their National Council of Civil Liberties (NNCL) book entitled *Positive Action for Women*, suggest the following courses of positive action:

Knowledge is power. Collect information. Use it to prove a pattern, not an individual grievance. If an interviewer asks inappropriate questions, for example, compare notes with other women and collate the results.

Construct a profile of the position of women in your department and use it to increase the awareness of your colleagues and superiors.

Contact other women pursuing a career in your organisation; isolation can make women feel personal failures, when, in fact, they may be the victims of the failure of employers to give them equal treatment.

Stand for office in your union. You need to break the male monopoly of workers' interests.

Union officials consider that women are a membership growth area, and even if they are a minority their voice counts. Demand information from employers – you need to know what jobs women do. Tackle inequalities, even if it makes you unpopular with male colleagues.

Sex discrimination and equal pay – taking your claim to law

Finally, if all else fails and you feel you are still being subjected to discrimination, then you can take your case to law under the Equal Pay Act or the Sex Discrimination Act. The best way to do this is to seek advice from either your union, the NCCL, and/or the EOC. An EOC leaflet contains the following statement:

> 'Are you thinking of making a complaint about sex discrimi-nation or equal pay? If you are we can help. We can help you to use these two Acts of Parliament ... Women and men too have the right to take their own complaints to an Industrial Tribunal or a court. ... Why not ask us?'

Don't try and go it alone. Use the expert bodies to support and advise you.

As already emphasised in Chapter 3, it's vital that you ensure that you are to receive a fair salary at the job interview or acceptance stage. Never be satisfied with or accept a salary level below what you and your job position warrant.

Women on the whole (including those in management and administrative positions) not only earn on average less than men but also complain about their pay far less than men do. One of the reasons for this is that women often feel grateful (and sometimes a little amazed) at the managerial levels they have reached and are more concerned with job satisfaction than with pay. This is a great mistake, as it not only perpetuates the wage differentials between men and women but also keeps women in positions of limited authority and power – the truth being that a high salary is usually always equated with more organisational power.

Sometimes, of course, employers play on these female attitudes towards pay. I met one woman who had been an Acting Area Manager for six months but had neither been given an Area Manager's salary or even an assistant. Her boss was testing her by making her do the job of her male predecessor on less pay and with less help and support. He was in fact saying, 'Prove to me you can do the job twice as well as a man, on less pay and without complaining, and eventually the permanent position *may* be yours.' In the end, having almost reached breaking point, she assertively de-manded her rights in terms of pay and assistance and somewhat to her surprise she got them straight away (wishing she'd asserted her rights six months earlier!).

The other difficulty that women workers have faced in the past is that no more than 10% of the total workforce is covered by job evaluation schemes and most females are in single-sex jobs where there are only a few men doing similar work. The same holds true for women in management positions (especially those in newly-created jobs) where there are no male managers in the same sort of jobs with whom they can compare themselves in terms of pay. However, the Equal Pay (Amendment) Regulations, which became law in 1984, allow women workers to claim the same pay and conditions as male colleagues doing totally different work, as long as the two jobs are of equal value in terms of such factors as training, decision-making, and physical and mental effort. These changes in the law were forced on a reluctant UK Government by the EEC and could have far-reaching effects. The EOC are backing a number of test cases, including women machinists in the furniture industry who are asking for parity with male upholsterers.

Taking all this into account, you owe it to those women who will follow you *not* to tolerate unfair pay or sex discrimination of any kind, and to use the support systems to help you fight your claim.

SUMMARY

- Identify the pressure sources in your life and your own stress symptoms as well as symptoms in others.

- Do something constructive to eliminate as far as possible your stressors and learn to control your stressful situations and redirect them to your own advantage.

- Set aside short periods in the day to carry out your own relaxation routine.

- Whenever you feel you are a victim of prejudice and discrimination, confront the individual (male or female) concerned in an assertive way and let your opinions be known.

- *Never ignore* sexual harassment – stop it before it becomes a pattern. Make your feelings known to the offender. Do not feel guilty and do not 'go it alone'. Get support from your colleagues. If the harassment persists, approach your union representative and/or follow the guidelines for coping successfully listed in this chapter.

● Take the initiative yourself and, with the support of female colleagues, work out your own positive action programme in your own organisation.

● As a final resort, if you feel you have been subjected to discrimination, then take your case to an Industrial Tribunal or to law under the Equal Pay Act or Sex Discrimination Act. Always seek union advice and/or advice and support from the EOC and NCCL.

CHAPTER 7

Dealing with the Home/ Work Conflict

'Women who are employed have two jobs since the
burden of domestic service and childcare is unrelieved
either by day care or other social agencies, or by the co-
operation of husbands. The invention of labour-saving
devices has had no appreciable effect on the duration,
even if it has affected the quality of their drudgery.'

Kate Millett, *Sexual Politics*, 1981

The majority of working women, especially those with
children, are far more easily affected by the burdens and
pressures of their home and childcare duties than are the
majority of working men. Even though as a professional
working woman you may be able to afford domestic and
childcare help, it is doubtful whether you will be totally
immune to the conflicting responsibilities associated with
running a home and a career.

You have already isolated your pressure sources at work
(Chapter 6). Now repeat exactly the same exercises, only this
time pinpoint your major pressure sources at home and in
your social life and set yourself an action plan, i.e. work out
constructive ways of dealing with these problems.

Table 7.1 lists the areas where female managers experience

Table 7.1 *Higher reported pressure levels at home and socially by 696 female managers (compared to 185 male managers)*

Earning more than spouse/partner.

Dependents (other than children) living at home.

Lack of domestic support at home.

Lack of emotional support at home.

Conflicting responsibilities associated with running a home and career.

Career-related dilemma concerning: whether to start a family, whether to marry/live with someone.

Being single and sometimes excluded from social and business events.

Being single and labelled an 'oddity'.

Source: Davidson and Cooper, *Stress and the Woman Manager*, 1983

higher home/social pressure levels than male managers. It will give you an indication of the most common pressure sources.

As well as finding practical solutions, discussing these potential problems in more depth will, hopefully, enable you to be more prepared for and better able to deal with some of home/work conflicts you may face.

For better or for worse – marriage and childbearing

In the survey I have just quoted, it was found that the highest level of stress for female managers concerned the career-related dilemma of whether to start a family. Even though almost one in three marriages ends in divorce, marriage is not on the decline and most people marry at least once in their lives. However, the profile of the professional woman who makes it to the top is often one of a woman who had remained single and childless and had chosen not to be faced with the dilemma of divided loyalties between career, husband and children. Although successful professional women often have common law/married partnerships with or without children, it is still the case that they are less likely to be married compared to their male counterparts, and if they are married they are less likely to have children. Only 57% of the 696 women managers in our survey were married compared to 75% of the 185 males. And of those women who were married, they had on average fewer children than the married male managers. Also twice the number of women were divorced or separated, i.e. 15·1% compared to 8·1% of the men.

There is no doubt that in most organisations today the married male manager is still viewed as an asset whereas the married female manager is looked on as a liability. One single woman in her late twenties illustrated this viewpoint:

> 'One of my managers was saying the other day about one of my male colleagues, "He's 29, he should be settling down and getting married." It's unlikely he'd say that about me. They like the men to be married and expect their wives to move around with them and make all the moving arrangements, etc. If I got married, though, they'd immediately assume I was no longer mobile and was likely to leave at any moment to have babies.'

In the majority of cases, women who have remained single without live-in partners, have usually made a conscious decision to do so. Often, they have not met a suitable partner who, in their opinion, would be able to accommodate their career and social lifestyles, and also by remaining single they are limiting the number of social roles they have to play and the degrees of role conflict.

The biggest complaint from single female managers is that people sometimes label them as a bit of an oddity. Dorothy was 30 years old before she decided to marry and she described her discomfort at being saddled with the 'left on the shelf' syndrome:

> 'It certainly did help me career-wise not to get married in my twenties. Besides my being able to pour all my energies into my job and being highly mobile, my employer took me much more seriously, especially once I'd passed my mid-twenties. Nevertheless, I got tired of the insinuations that there must be something wrong with me because I wasn't married. Remarks such as, "But Dorothy, you're so attractive, I can't understand why some man hasn't come along and whisked you down the aisle," were common. You

look around and see a lot of your contemporaries getting married and having children, and when I was feeling vulnerable there were times when I thought "Perhaps they're right, perhaps there *is* something wrong with me!" I don't think men who aren't married have quite the same pressure – they tend to be envied for their carefree bachelor status.'

Other detrimental effects of remaining single include being excluded from the business social network and not having a 'wife' at home to give domestic and social support:

'As a single home-owner (with a car and a garden), I work on average a 50-hour week at the office and take work home. I compete with male colleagues who, whilst working the same hours, enjoy clean clothes, prepared meals, clean homes and have someone at home to let in the gasman, decorators, repair men, etc. We tend to assume that the main problems facing women in management are the demands of the family/spouse. Believe me, being single and having a career is no push-over! If you can afford it, my advice is to pay someone to do your cleaning and ironing. If business entertaining is important to your career, then make it clear that you are content to be invited to dinner parties, etc alone and without a partner. You should also throw business dinner parties yourself and if preparation time is a problem use home caterers who bring the food to your house. It's not as expensive as it sounds.'

Is there ever a right time to have a baby?

Most women in interesting well-paid jobs are tending to postpone having their children until they are in their thirties. By the time a woman reaches her early thirties she is often beginning to establish herself in her career, and yet at the same time is reaching the older primigravida years in terms of childbearing. Decisions concerning marriage and/or child-bearing are major dilemmas for these women: 'How will it affect my career, lifestyle and relationships?' 'Should I take a break or return to work after maternity leave?' 'Will I be able to get a job if I quit?' These questions and doubts go through most women's minds.

Now that women usually have a choice about motherhood, it's interesting to analyse the reasons why the urge to have children is often so strong. Sociologists Robert and Rhona Rapoport proposed that having children makes people feel complete; it makes them immortal; it demonstrates their sense of altruism and responsibility; it increases the sources of love open to them, it gives the parents some power and influence over other human beings; and it is fun and creative.

Some women choose to have their children very early while others wait until they are relatively well established in their careers. Cathy Moulder and Pat Sheldon in their book *Back to Work – A Practical Guide for Women* advocate that there are advantages in both systems, but make the point that if a woman puts off having children until she is fully qualified and well known in her profession, she will probably find it much less unnerving to stage her comeback.

The other option is not to have children at all, but this can also have its problems. The idea that women want babies is propagated by our society and women who don't want babies (especially if they are married) tend to be viewed as being abnormal and selfish, and are often required to explain their motives.

Failing to do 'my duty'

'We have made a conscious decision *not* to have any children. When I was in my twenties, being a married career woman, most people just tended to assume that I was delaying starting a family until my career took off. Now, there is often the inference from male colleagues and relatives that I must be odd and selfish. One guy at work recently implied that I was obviously very materialistic and money meant more to me than children. It amazes me how even complete strangers such as taxi drivers feel they have the right to cross-examine you about "Why you're not doing your duty". I don't inquire of strangers or friends why they've *chosen* to have children! There's also tremendous pressure from parents and in-laws to present them with grandchildren – especially if you're an only child. My response to this type of goading is usually that at the present time we have decided not to have children and in our eyes it's far more of a selfish act to bring an unwanted child into the world.'

The golden rule, though, whether it involves a decision to get married or if you become pregnant, is always to make your future plans known to your employer. If you marry it is often wrongly assumed by employers that it means the end of your career plans and that your sights are now firmly set on buying maternity clothes and nappies. As soon as your bulge is noticed, you are often not expected to return after maternity leave, even if you've stated otherwise. Leafing through a recent American edition of *Vogue* magazine, my eye was caught by an advertisement showing a photograph of a woman holding a briefcase, obviously pregnant, and wearing a smart dress suit. The ad read:

> '*Maternity Business Suits and Dresses* – Classic business clothing, traditionally styled for the pregnant working woman who must maintain a professional image throughout her pregnancy. For catalogue, including 22 fabric swatches, send $3, refundable with order, to . . .'

I wonder how long it will be before our own clothing industry view the pregnant British businesswoman as an important marketing target! Certainly, it was wonderful to see that in the first edition of the UK magazine *Working Woman*, the special fashion offer of the month was a designer maternity outfit for the professional, pregnant working woman.

Planning your pregnancy

A close girlfriend and work colleague decided to have her first baby at the age of 30 and planned the conception to the exact month so that the birth would coincide with the University summer break. She even used a special douche in the hope of having a boy. She conceived in the planned month – but had a girl! My friend also planned for the impending addition very carefully. She returned to work after maternity leave having arranged before the birth for a childminder to look after the baby on the two days each week when she had heavy teaching commitments; her husband's flexi-time meant he could look after the baby for one day and on the other two days she brought her to work, and as we shared an office I was able to keep an eye on the child for the few hours her mother was away giving tutorials.

But this type of precise planning and work flexibility is the exception rather than the rule. Most women take between six months and a year to conceive, and over 10% of couples in this country have infertility problems. If you plan to delay having a baby until your late twenties or thirties (especially if you suspect you may have problems in conceiving), without meaning to sound alarmist, it's a good idea to go and have a gynaecological check-up and discuss your queries with a sympathetic doctor.

Knowing your maternity rights

In my experience, the majority of working women are unaware of the legal details concerning pregnancy and maternity rights and tend to find out *after* they become pregnant. Unless your pregnancy means that you are unable to do your job properly or your work may harm the foetus, as in the case of X-rays, and as long as you have been working for your employer full-time for six months, then there are no grounds to sack you. If you are sacked, it is now considered unfair dismissal and you have right of appeal to an Industrial Tribunal.

You also have the right to be reinstated in your job for up to 29 weeks after the birth of your baby, provided that you:

1. Have been working for your employer for at least two years by the beginning of the eleventh week before the baby is due.

2. Have carried on working up until the beginning of the eleventh week before the week in which the baby is due.

3. Have informed your employer that you intend to exercise your right to return to work at least three weeks before you leave work; and at least one week before you intend returning to work.

4. Provide your employer with a certificate signed by your doctor or midwife giving the estimated date of the baby's birth.

5. If you do not return to work after 29 weeks from the birth of your baby you forfeit your job *unless* you are permitted a four-week extension due to ill health; or your employer delays your return for up to four weeks if you are informed by the end of the 29th week; or if there is any industrial disruption.

The law states that the job to which you return must be the same job you were doing according to your contract of employment. In her book, *How to Survive as a Working Mother*, Lesley Garner advises you to check the wording of your contract carefully in order to clarify any possible misunderstandings in advance. For example, if your contract simply describes you as a Marketing Manager, you may not wish to return to a job marketing cosmetics if your job used to be marketing industrial chemicals. You should make sure you read all the relevant Government leaflets as soon as you know you are pregnant in order to ascertain your employment rights and maternity benefits. These can be obtained from your local DHSS office.

Interestingly, a 1982 report by the EOC entitled *Parenthood in the Balance* outlines how Britain's mothers and fathers are lagging behind many of their European colleagues in maternity and paternity pay and conditions. The report says that Britain is almost alone among 14 countries in insisting on a two-year working requirement with the same employer before maternity pay can be given. It calls for an immediate increase in the maternity grant, the introduction of paid paternity leave, and the removal of restrictions on the eligibility for maternity leave.

After the baby – The Big Decision

'The only barrier I see career-wise is if at some point I have a child. It worries me that generally we don't have senior women coming back after having children – there is little encouragement. The male managers all seem to have non-working wives. I want to work and just take maternity leave. I worry that even doing that, having a young child might be held against me.'

Many women do return to work after maternity leave and the reasons are numerous, ranging from career enjoyment and advancement to financial necessity and self-esteem. It is important to weigh up the pros and cons carefully before deciding to take a career break. The protective home environment may indeed seem a welcome relief after years of working in a competitive, high pressure job!

Also, waiting to have a first child until your thirties is, for some women, more of a planned commitment as far as energies and time is concerned. One of the most senior women in a large multinational organisation gave up a £20,000+ a year job when she had her first child at the age of 32 and said:

'Whatever I do, I like to do 100%, and after my baby was born I decided that as I had given all my energies to my job for more than 10 years, now I would give them to her. I have no regrets and will return to work sometime in the next few years.'

In terms of sheer economics, of course, professional women who leave their jobs after the birth of their babies are a great loss to their organisations, both in terms of years of training, experience and talent as well as the costs involved in replacing them. Thus it is encouraging to note that, with the increase in the number of women entering professional and managerial positions, some organisations have taken positive action to overcome this problem and have introduced experimental re-entry schemes. These schemes vary in their stipulations from offering part-time work (including working from home and job-sharing schemes) to giving complete work breaks for a number of years with periodical refresher training courses during weekends and holidays.

Considering that the average break from the workforce for *all* women is about seven years – which accounts for 16–19%

of the time between the ages of 20 and 59 – the working lives of mothers are reduced but not dramatically curtailed. The majority of the professional women I have interviewed maintained that they would welcome the introduction of part-time work and re-entry schemes, wishing eventually to return to work after a break. You must never dismiss the possibility of initiating similar schemes in your own company, as illustrated by this woman computer operator:

'I was pregnant with my first child and although I'd told Personnel I would be taking maternity leave and then returning to work, in truth I wanted to spend more time with the baby – after all, I was 34 and had waited a long time for this baby, having put my career first. I then heard about another woman in another department who had come back part-time for a couple of years after the birth of her child and was about to take up full-time employment again. So I thought "If she can do it, why can't I?" I took the idea to Personnel and, although it took some fighting, I won and am now working part-time. The interesting thing is that more and more women are now demanding the same rights in our company and so it looks as if it may well become normal practice. I do think more women should fight for their rights on this one, and point out the economic benefits to the organisation.'

The implications of taking a career break

The major hazards associated with taking a career break are first of all potential feelings of boredom and under-stimulation combined with loss of status. (Housewives in this country are now a minority and tend to be saddled with undeserved low status – the 'I'm *only* a housewife' syndrome.) Secondly, the longer you stay out of the workforce, the harder it is to re-enter at the same level. Thirdly, the cocooned home environment can result in loss of confidence and a fear of coping with the pressures of working life.

Nevertheless, women are unfairly penalised by the majority of employers for taking a career break. Margery Povall, in the

MSC report *Managing or Removing the Career Break*, highlights that unlike the maternity break, breaks initiated by employers are accepted as being inevitable, essential, or for the greater good. She goes on to state:

> 'We sometimes talk as though it is only women with children who have breaks from employment. This is, of course, not true. Many employees have breaks of one kind or another from their normal job. Some are transferred elsewhere for a period either to deal with a crisis or to give them wider experience. Others may be sent away for training or education – the one year at a management training centre for the high flyer. Some leave one employer to go off to another organisation, and may later return. In some industries such as the computer industry, it is seen as quite reasonable to do this. Some in the past went on military service and others now are made redundant in their field at an early age. All these people have needed to be reintegrated to some extent when they returned to work. None of these breaks is seen as an insuperable obstacle, and many are seen as positive. Employees are seen as coming back with new knowledge, confidence, experience.'

A long overdue emphasis is now being made on the numerous business skills involved in running a home and taking care of children, and as I emphasised at the beginning of this book you must never underestimate these talents. However, if you do intend to return to work full-time eventually, it is advisable to keep in touch with your specialisation by reading, attending refresher courses, studying part-time, or taking on part-time job-sharing or occasional freelance work (which you may be able to carry out based at home). My own mother had four children and when the first three were pre-school age, she worked part-time as a physiotherapist while my two sisters and I went to nursery school. When my youngest sister was born, she decided to stop work, stay at home for five years and use the time as an opportunity to get qualifications for a completely different occupation. She studied for a University diploma (part-time) and then went on to gain an Open University degree – today, she is a full-time college lecturer.

Returning to work after the break

Re-entering the workforce after a few years break can prove a harrowing prospect. There are a number of courses available which seek to meet the needs of women at this vital stage. The best-known are the Wider Opportunities for Women (WOW) courses sponsored throughout the country by the Manpower Services Commission. (You can write to the MSC for details.)

The aim of WOW courses is to help women returnees to make realistic and informed choices of occupational or training plans, based on local labour-market opportunities and an assessment of their own skills, and to instil the skills and self-confidence necessary to carry out these plans. The total course takes six weeks and the MSC recommends that the course content should include eight token days individual job sampling, refresher sessions of basic skills, group visits, discussion sessions focusing on dual role problems, information-giving sessions on work-related topics, self-assessment, job search and self-presentation skills.

Barbara Douglas, a psychologist, has completed an investigation into the stresses experienced by women who are looking after children at home during a work break as well as those of working mothers. I asked Barbara what sort of successful tactics were used by the women returners she had interviewed:

'The majority of women returning to work were asked at their interviews what childcare arrangements they had made, so it's a good idea to have that one sorted out beforehand. Moreover, women who had plenty of back-up in respect to childcare were at a distinct advantage compared to women who just relied on one person such as a relative, who could be vulnerable to sickness, etc. Many of the women, when asked what advice they would give to other women wishing to return to work, said, "to have a supportive husband," although nearly every one of them did far more in the house and on childcare duties than their husbands. And, not surprisingly, the most common pressure for the returning working mother was *guilt* about the harm they might be inflicting on their children. In fact, it was the women's mothers and mothers-in-law who instigated and facilitated most of this "guilt trip".'

137

The working mother – coping with guilt

In *Superwoman*, in the section dealing with how to be a working wife and mother, Shirley Conran asserts:

> 'It is important that you shouldn't feel guilty about working – and this is impossible. You have been conditioned to feel guilty. Accept it. Children instinctively know that your guilt about your work is your Achilles heel and will use it, when they are bored, or cross, to have a crack at you.'

It was the child psychologist, John Bowlby, who played a large part in stirring up guilt feelings in working mothers by his post-war studies on the effects of maternal deprivation and the perils of being separated from your mother when young. Although his research has been invalidated by numerous subsequent studies, his effects have been long-lasting. A major reason for this was that politically it was useful ammunition for governments to use in order to validate the withdrawal of nursery facilities and get women back into the home, away from the 'male jobs' they had taken over during the war, thus allowing men once more to occupy their 'rightful place' in the workforce. During the 1950s, women's magazines which during the war years had been adorned with working women in overalls were now full of images of the perfect homemaker in the kitchen wearing a frilly white apron and with a wide-eyed toddler in tow. Female labour tends to be ping-ponged from the workforce back into the home, depending on the political and economic climate of the day.

Even though you may find it impossible to feel guilt-free about being a working mother, it's worth reminding yourself every so often of the latest research findings. For example, some recent research published by the US National Academy of Sciences showed that children need not suffer if their mother has a paid job and ought to reassure any working woman who feels guilty about leaving her child. (*Children of Working Parents*, National Academy Press, Washington DC, 1983.) The study found 'no conclusive research evidence to suggest that the mother's employment *per se* (by single mothers or mothers in two-parent families) has consistent, direct effects, either positive or negative, on children's development and educational outcomes.' Furthermore, it was other variables such as family structure, income, individual characteristics of the child (such as sex, handicap, or age), mother's education and attitudes towards employment and housework, and the availability of support services which seemed to be far more important in shaping a child's development.

It is also a myth that working mothers are a liability as far as high absenteeism is concerned. This has been illustrated by research compiled by the EOC and included in their leaflet entitled *Sickness Absence from Work*. A woman with dependent children working full-time takes, on average, nearly 13 days' sickness absence each year. The average for all full-time women workers is 10 days compared to nine for men. Women tend to take time off more often, but for shorter periods. The best absence records are for part-timers, who are predominantly female. Those who work 10 hours or less take off about 5·5 days a year and the figure for those working 11 to 29 hours is 6·8 days. Absence for personal and domestic reasons is much less than for sickness.

Childcare options

Part-time or job-sharing work in professional, administrative and managerial jobs are rare and so the majority of women returning to these professions after maternity leave or a career break will probably be working full-time. Unless you can rely on help from relatives who live nearby you will have to entrust your child to a stranger's care. In *How to Survive as a Working Mother*, Lesley Garner describes the inadequate childcare facilities in this country by quoting the latest figures:

'At the last count there were 30,333 registered childminders providing places for 91,878 children. There were 27,000 places in local authority day nurseries. There were 2,400 places in work-place nurseries and crèches and there were 22,000 places in private day nurseries. That makes 143,278 places in registered day care for small children of working mothers. But 850,000 children under five have working mothers.'

139

In their book, *Back to Work*, Cathy Moulder and Pat Sheldon give detailed accounts of the various childcare facilities one can use, plus the average cost and dozens of useful addresses. Below is a summary of their recommendations and options:

A full-time nanny/au pair: The most expensive solution to the working mother's childcare problem but an effective stand-in for you. Nannies attend either on a daily or live-in basis, and you can advertise for a nanny/mother's help in *The Lady* or *Nursery World* or use an agency. The other alternative is an au pair, but the disadvantage here is that they tend to stay with a family for only about six months on average.

Nurseries/play groups/crèches: Day nurseries or crèches run by local authorities are still very scarce in Britain but you can try to apply for a place for your child by contacting your area health visitor or Social Services Department. There are also private nursery schools and some Universities and a small number of companies offer crèche facilities which you can find out about by contacting your local Women's Centre if you have one or your Citizens Advice Bureau. Playgroups usually only take children between the ages of three and five for a few hours in the day and your local authority health department and planning committee should be able to provide you with a list of groups in your area.

Childminders: By law *all* childminders should be registered with the Social Services Department which will have checked the minder and their home. You usually leave your child at the home of the childminder, who is usually only allowed to look after a maximum of three children at a time. (Make sure your childminder *is* registered.)

For many working mothers who find satisfactory pre-school childcare for their children, the problems often begin when the children start school and need looking after for a few hours after school ends. Many parents use non-working friends or pay someone to meet their children from school and take care of them until one or other of the parents returns from work. Some schools now operate after-school caring schemes and you can find out about these by contacting your local education authority.

Getting partners to share domestic work

Cross-cultural research findings have shown that women managers who have children (especially young children at home) spend more time with their children than male managers do, find themselves less able to relax at the end of the day, and are even more susceptible to feelings of guilt, role conflict, work overload, tiredness and ill-health. (It should be also emphasised that both single and married women managers are more likely to take on heavier responsibilities concerning taking care of elderly parents.) I once interviewed a very senior female executive whose joint income with her husband was over £45,000 a year and yet she had no help in the house and did everything herself because she felt she ought to be doing all the work in order to prove she was a good wife and mother.

Although the majority of women I have talked to still maintain they do more home duties than their partners, there are signs that a new breed of husbands married to professional women is causing a shift in the distribution of home responsibilities more towards sharing. Even so, as pointed out by Ann Oakley in her book *Subject Women*, men tend to be very selective in the chores they choose to do. These tend to be creative tasks such as cooking and shopping or 'masculine' jobs such as home improvements, cutting the lawn, taking out the rubbish, etc. I have yet to meet many men who admit to cleaning out the toilet bowl regularly or washing dirty nappies!

Gaining co-operation – a home duties audit

After speaking at a joint Industrial Society and Guardian Women's Page conference for working mothers entitled Divided Loyalties, one of the female participants asked me:

'It's O.K. for the lucky women who have partners and children who do help in the house, but how does one go about changing the likes of my husband whose mother did

141

everything for him and who has expected me to do the same? My children are of little help either, even though they are in their early teens. I know it's partly my fault but how do I go about getting any help, change or *action*?'

My response was that she should resort to using assertion skills and begin a plan of action. I suggested that she should choose a time when all the family were together to announce that she was dissatisfied with the distribution of household tasks and wasn't prepared to continue doing the brunt of the work. During the previous week she should carry out a *home duties audit* whereby she monitored the number of hours spent on different household tasks by herself and other members of the family. These facts and figures should be produced during this session, and discussion and negotiation should then follow as to how these tasks could be more evenly distributed.

A good idea is to do what my mother did, and pin up a home duties rota for each day of the week in the kitchen. My sisters and I hated it, of course, but it did us no harm and unpopular chores could be rotated. The employment of domestic help of some kind, including perhaps someone to do the ironing (one of the most disliked household chores) could also be rationally discussed during these negotiations. Although the going may be tough, *do not* give in – equality at home is as important as equality in the workplace. Take heart from recent research in Sweden which has shown that the men most involved in childcare are married to women in well-paid, high status jobs who are *more assertive*. Also, it's never too late to rock the *status quo* in your household. One middle-aged office administrator who attended an assertion course I was running described how she took the initiative with her family after 15 years!

'I've been working for the past 10 years and have a husband and a 16-year-old son. I've always done everything for them in the house as I felt the usual guilt about not being a good wife and mother because I worked. Also, I felt they expected me to wash, cook, clean, iron, sew, etc for them. To be honest, I hate housework and am not that keen on cooking. Thinking about it, I have felt resentful doing it all over the years, although I've rarely mentioned it. Perhaps the worst time is when I get home from work. I arrive home last feeling tired to find the two of them sitting in front of the TV waiting for me to come home and set the table, cook tea for them and wash up! Last night, though, was different.

'I arrived home, said a quick hello to them both then went into the back room, put my feet up and had a relaxing cup of coffee. After about half an hour, they both came in with "What about tea mum?"

'I can't pretend my heart wasn't thumping hard, but I kept a calm, firm voice and replied, "I don't feel like tea tonight, so go ahead and make something for yourself – the fridge is full."

'To my amazement all hell didn't break loose; certainly, they looked a little surprised, but they *did* cook their own tea and I resisted the temptation to go into the kitchen in response to their cries for help. The relief and satisfaction I felt was immense and there are going to be more changes in the distribution of household tasks in our house. And I'm going to start practising assertion skills at work too.

'I know last night might seem an insignificant episode, but to me it was a great milestone which had taken me 10 years to cross!'

Choosing the right partner

There is no doubt, that for the working professional woman whose job may involve irregular hours and travel away from home, having a partner who gives both domestic, social and psychological support is of vital importance.

Although in 1980 only 8% of wives earned as much as or more than their employed husbands, managerial and professional women obviously feature strongly in this small category. Interestingly, earning more than one's spouse or partner was for some women managers in our large-scale survey a source of relationship conflict (see Table 7.1). Obviously, there is no easy solution to this one and by-passing one's partner in relation to job status and salary seems to be a potential problem area which particularly affects older couples.

It is always possible to seek solutions and find social support, as it is with the majority of potential problems mentioned throughout this book. One couple in their mid-forties described their own personal solution to this source of conflict in their marriage:

'When I became Head of a large school, I did notice soon after that things had become strained between my husband and myself. I couldn't really put my finger on it, but I felt he resented me in some way and he kept making odd remarks about the money I was bringing in and how he might as well take early retirement (he's a social worker). In the end we sat down and really thrashed it out. It turned out that he felt uneasy about me earning so much more than he did. He said it made him feel inadequate and a failure.

'I told him it made no difference to me who earned what as long as we were happy, and that in my eyes his job was just as worthwhile and important as mine. Things are much better now and they've been helped by making friends with another couple who are in a similar position. We all give each other support in a strange kind of way and it also makes us feel less odd and unusual. It's all to do with conditioning of course, but I don't think it's as big an issue with young couples.'

Another very real source of potential conflict for working couples is the job mobility issue. Although in the past few years there has been a trend for professionals to resist enforced mobility, it appears that compared to our European counterparts, we British still tend to be pretty flexible. In 1980, for example, a survey by an international management magazine found that the country with the highest percentage of managers (i.e. 56%) who said that they would relocate if asked was Britain.

The job mobility issue is a particular dilemma for dual career couples, and unfortunately it is still common for both organisations and individuals to assume that the man's career takes precedent over the woman's. This type of attitude can undoubtedly place a strain on relationships, as well as hamper a woman's career development. A recent survey was carried out by a team at Sheffield University on the effects that job changes have on individuals and it included 806 female and 1,498 male managers and professionals. According to one of the researchers, Dr Beverly Alban Metcalfe, many of the women referred to job changes which had been imposed on them because their male partners had to move location for career reasons. These women expressed a degree of resentment at the assumption that a woman should move for her husband's career advancement, but not vice versa.

From my own research findings, the couples who seem to cope best with the dual career mobility problem are those who discuss the problem together and make *fair compromises*. Indeed, there are indications that for a growing number of couples, the compromise reached is often one whereby they opt for the 'weekend relationship' and accept separation during the week. Fortunately, Britain seems to be following the American model of looking more closely at this mobility issue and questioning whether it is really necessary to uproot managers and executives every few years.

Finally, when it comes to ensuring contentment on the home front, the same message has been echoed time and time again: 'Choose your partner carefully!' Mary Kenny, in *Women × Two – How to Cope with a Double Life*, outlines many of the qualities which make an ideal working woman's husband:

'The ideal husband, then, is not just someone who is helpful, supportive and mature; not just someone who is not competing for the same things and at the same time as his wife; not just someone who is flexible, uses his initiative, and is ready to turn his hand to anything; not just someone who gets on with his mother and encourages his wife; not just a selfish egotist, and not just a yes-man. It's someone who is all these things and who on top of that has an acutely tuned sensitivity to just how far he should go in encouraging her, in helping her, in sharing roles. Perhaps it's not, after all, surprising that the ladies who possess such specimens should be so wondrously grateful, so warmly appreciative, of the supermen in their lives.'

SUMMARY

● If you can afford it, especially if you live alone, pay someone to do your cleaning and ironing.

● If you are unattached, don't allow yourself to become isolated when it comes to business socialising.

● If you marry or become pregnant, let your future plans be known to your employer to stop inaccurate assumptions being made.

● If you decide to start a family, find out details about your legal pregnancy and maternity rights as an employee, as well as your entitled maternity benefits. If you are planning to return to work after maternity leave, you will need to organise childcare arrangements even before your baby is born. Also, check your contract of employment before you take maternity leave to ensure your chances of returning to the same job.

● It is important to weigh the pros and cons carefully before deciding to take a complete career break.

● *Stop feeling guilty* about being a working mother. The very latest research shows that children do not suffer just because their mother has a paid job.

● If you take a break and intend eventually to return to work full- or part-time, try and keep in touch with your specialisation and don't be afraid to use this time to do extra part-time study. Before going back to work, consider attending one of the courses such as WOW which are aimed specifically at helping women returners. Emphasise the business skills involved in running a home at your job interview.

● Do not try and be superwoman. Negotiate with your partner and children (if they are old enough) about a fair distribution of household tasks. Prepare a home duties audit and, if necessary, work rotas. Don't give in and always be assertive about your rights. Finances permitting, employ domestic help.

- When faced with dual career mobility problems, discuss the issue in depth with your partner and make fair compromises.

- If you haven't already – choose your partner carefully!

CHAPTER 8

Recipes for Success

'Women, in general, do not differ from men, in general, in the ways in which they administer the management process ... the disproportionately low numbers of women in management can no longer be explained away by the contention that women practise a different brand of management from that practised by men.'

S.M. Donnell and J. Hall, *Men and Women Managers: A Significant Case of No Significant Difference*, Organizational Dynamics, Spring, 1980

In this book I have tried to offer constructive guidelines to women who wish to follow a successful, professional career in business, management and administration. The importance of women acting as role models has already been emphasised, and so as a final chapter I thought it appropriate to present the personal experiences of five women. I chose to interview these particular women because they were all different as far as their ages, family backgrounds, education, home/marital situations, and types of managerial jobs were concerned. They each describe their own life and work histories, and in so doing illustrate that there is no one fixed route into the world of business and management. With talent and know-how, the way is open to all women who wish to pursue it.

Sheila J. Needham – Managing Director of Needham Printers Limited

Date of birth	22nd June 1937
Marital Status	Single
Education	Sutton High School, G.P.D.S.T. Sutton, Surrey. Mrs Hoster's Secretarial Training College, London SW7.

Career

From October 1955	Six secretarial and personal assistant positions in London, New York and California for BBC, Merchant Bank, Oil Company, Architect, Civil Engineers and Quantity Surveyor.
February 1965	Director and Company Secretary of Offset Lithographers and Stationers Company, London. Then made:
November 1971	Executive Director and Manager.
March 1974	Founder and Managing Director of Needham Printers Limited, general commercial printers: first at 12 Artillery Lane, London E1 7LS; moved 19th January 1981 to Titchfield House, 69–85, Tabernacle Street, London EC2A 4BA.

Other Activities

Farringdon Ward Club (a City of London Ward Club)	On committee 1972 to date. President 30th April 1984.
NE District London Printing Industries Association (part of the British Printing Industries Federation)	Committee member: 1977–1981. Hon. Secretary: 1979–1981. President: 1981.
London Printing Industries Association	Council member 1978–1981.
The Institute of Directors	Member: December 1983 to date.
Christian Responsibility in Public Affairs (part of International Christian Leadership)	Committee member: 1973 to date.

Freeman of the City of London	July 1977.
The Worshipful Company of Stationers and Newspaper Makers	Freeman: 1979. Liveryman: July 1981 to date.

In addition I have served on a number of charitable committees in the past including: The Sail Training Association, London Young Members Committee, YWCA, Earls Court Redevelopment Committee, Mildmay Mission Hospital Advisory Council.

Family background

I am the first born and have a brother. My father was the Chief Surveyor of a City insurance company. He would not let my mother go out to work, so I'm not sure he ever expected me to take up a serious career. He thought I would marry. Both my brother and I went to public schools and were expected to do well – I was always a slogger rather than a success and had to work harder than my brother.

When I left school, I rebelled against going to University. This upset my school, but not my parents. They simply wanted me to be happy. My school's question was, 'After you have finished your secretarial course, what are you going to do?' They certainly did not understand my answer, 'Be a secretary.' I was good at physics and I knew my father would have liked me to become a research scientist, but I suddenly felt that wasn't what I wanted to do – succeed in the scientific world. At the time I had a bad stammer so I thought that teaching was out of the question.

Work and life profile

After finishing secretarial college I went to work for the BBC and was totally happy being a secretary. For the next nine years I had half a dozen different secretarial jobs which included working for a merchant bank, an oil company, an architectural practice and a civil engineering company. I really enjoyed these jobs as they enabled me to travel and work in

150

places like New York and California. Looking back on those times now, I realise I gained a lot from those experiences. Then, in my late twenties, I decided I wanted a greater challenge. I took a job as Personal Assistant to a quantity surveyor. I saw that this job would give me more scope and opportunity. My new boss turned out to be very much my mentor. He sent me abroad to do research and expected me to do things that normally I wouldn't have had the confidence to do. He pushed me and believed in me even though I found it all a bit nerve-racking. I didn't disappoint him though.

After I'd been working for him for a year, my boss decided to set up a small printing company of his own. It started out very small and as his PA I did all of the arrangements: employed the staff, found customers, etc. From the beginning, he made me a Director of the company so I would stay on working as his PA/Secretary. As the company grew it took up more and more of my time. I was working very hard and in effect doing two full-time jobs: running the company and being his secretary. Consequently, one day my boss took me to lunch and put a proposition to me: either I was to remain his PA *or* run the printing company. I was then 32 and I decided the right move would be to accept the job of running the printers. But my boss did not like the decision. He did not want to lose me as his PA/Secretary! In fact he interviewed women for nine months before he eventually appointed someone to be my replacement.

I was now free to move the printing company away from my boss's office into larger premises. Initially, my boss made things very difficult for me. Whilst he did not give me the authority to make company decisions, he did not have the *time* (or make the time) to make them himself. He had too many other business activities. His new secretary and I quickly became friends. She used to ring me up and tell me when he was on his way to see me. This annoyed him.

When I got engaged I decided to leave the job. Six weeks before the wedding date the engagement was broken. As my boss had not started to do anything about replacing me, my job was still open and it was easy for me to stay on.

But I continued to be frustrated with my boss's refusal to make decisions I felt should be made or allowing me to make

151

them myself. I decided I had to get out and do something else. So I went to an agency to ask advice. They told me to look in *The Times* for suitable job positions. I subsequently applied for the post of Managing Director of a small employment agency. It was over nine years since my last interview and I was terrified! It was a shock to be offered the job at twice the salary I was getting. But, I turned the position down simply because I found I loved the world of printing too much to leave it. Next I offered to buy my boss out of the printing company. He refused to consider the idea!

I was feeling pretty despondent by the whole thing. I returned from a holiday in Morocco with a bad case of dysentry which meant two weeks' sick leave. For the first week I was very poorly indeed but during my gradual recovery in the second week, I wrote a feasibility study for setting up my own new printing company. I found an accountant who was willing to back me financially and ten years ago I started Needham Printers Limited from scratch. I secured some premises and took on three staff. My initial work came from my backer's practice. I carefully didn't work for any of my old customers at the other company. Today I have new, larger premises and a staff of 25. Business is healthy and growing.

I think being a woman has helped me in some ways. Getting customers, for example, has been easier for me as people are curious about dealing with a female Managing Director, especially in the male-dominated world of printing. I must admit, some customers do tend to assume that I must have inherited the business from my father. On the other hand, you do get people who test you to see if you really do know about the technologies of print. They wouldn't do that with a man in my position. I tend to smile to myself when that happens. There's a lot of pressure in the printing industry as there are always deadlines to meet. I have had to learn to 'switch off', especially when I get home.

In the early days, some men may have found it hard working for me because I was a woman. Now I always ask senior men at their interview about how they will feel about this and ask them also to discuss it with their wives. So far, it hasn't created any problems. The men say that it's different working for a woman but won't say in what way! I think many men fear that a woman will be too emotional and it can be difficult to persuade them that your responses are rational, *not* emotional.

Handling home/work conflicts

I tend to work late rather than take work home, as I like to keep my work and home life separate. I suppose if I'd dedicated everything to my job I may have been more successful, but the overall quality of life is important to me. I live on my own and have never married. I do have someone who comes to do my cleaning and ironing. I think it's essential and it makes such a difference. When I take customers out to lunch I often get remarks such as, 'But Sheila, you are so feminine!' I'm not quite sure what they expected and I don't see why a woman in my job shouldn't be feminine. I do find that, socially, the men I meet of my age group (especially if they're not married) often feel threatened by me. I occasionally get advances from married men as they seem to have the confidence (and possibly the security, because they are married) to be comfortable with me. However, I could not approve of a relationship with a married man and I don't think I am a threat to men's wives. The men who work for me know I have got boyfriends and that I've got an active social life outside of work. In particular I love cooking, throwing dinner parties and going to the theatre.

Given your time over again – would you change anything?

I'm not sure. I never thought of myself in terms of having a career, I wasn't ambitious and I didn't plan my career. I always thought I'd marry and have children and it wasn't until the age of 35 after a broken engagement that, as a late starter, I began to plan a career rather than just having a job.

Advice to other women

Be yourself and get on with your job without being aggressive. Men can only relate to you if you act naturally. I'm straight-forward and direct in my interactions with people and I think that approach works. Remember that some men will be initially nervous of you. I used to assume that a man running a company would know a lot more than I do and I was embarrassed by my secretarial background. Now I realise I often know as much as they do!

If you decide to set up your own business you must gain some financial knowledge, how to do a cash flow, charging, etc. You should also know something about the industry you are going into. Buy the skills you don't have. Respect your employees' skills and they will respect yours. There is no need to compete with them. Most of all you must *enjoy* building up your business. Realise that you will have to put in far more hours than if you were working for someone else. But, working for yourself, you will never have to endure conflicts with the boss and your enthusiasm will probably cause you to feel less tired.

Barbara Blyth – Head of Music, Granada Television

Citizenship	Canadian & British
Marital Status	Married

Education

1969	Royal Conservatory of Toronto ARCT (Associateship)
1970	Alfred University, New York, BA (cum laude) in Fine Arts
1978	Polytechnic of Central London, Diploma in Arts & Leisure Administration

Career

1971–1972	Arrived in London and spent a year travelling around Britain and doing temporary secretarial work
1972–1974	Transatlantic Records Ltd, London Held three main posts: Production Coordinator Classical Promotions Officer Copyright Officer

1974–1976	Riverside Recordings Ltd, London Trainee Tape Operator – by end of stay was handling 16-track sessions of all types of music as well as running their 'Copy Shop'
1976–1977	Transatlantic Records Ltd, London Rejoined this company as Marketing Label Manager Later made Creative Services Manager
1979–1980	Blyth & Hackel (Arts Management) Ltd Started agency with colleague. We handled classical and jazz musicians and functioned more or less as a conventional agency, obtaining bookings for our artists, negotiating contracts and chasing up payments for work done.
1980–present	Granada Television Head of Music My job encompasses the commissioning of composers to write music for programmes, contracting all musical performers, organising music sessions, dealing with arrangers, copyists and contractors. It is my job to see that the terms of the agreement between the Musicians' Union and the ITV companies are carried out in practice. Music copyright in general and its application to broadcasting, cable and video is assuming a larger and larger portion of my work as new areas of exploitation of television programmes become possible.

Family background

I was born in Canada and I've got two sisters, one five years older and one five years younger. My mother worked as a secretary (in a law office) before she got married, then when my younger sister was 12 she couldn't stand being at home any longer so she brushed up her secretarial skills and got a full-time job working for the Ontario Government. She's got a brilliant business mind and did very well, quickly moving away from secretarial work into a managerial post in charge of archives using system computers. My mother is really quite a feminist in her own way although she'd blanch at the idea. Her parents sent her to University, even though it was during the

155

Depression and she always felt strongly that girls should be educated.

My father worked for a large insurance business and tended to keep his ideas about his daughters' futures to himself. However, my mother's story is that he didn't particularly care if any of his daughters had a University education. I must say though that now he's very proud of us all.

I think that my decision to follow a career in music was due to my mother encouraging my talent, and my father did have a dance band when he was younger so there was a musical background in our family. Even so, neither of them were pushy at all, although we were all expected to do well at school, that was 'our job'. I remember a saying from my mother was, 'No Blyth girl is ever going to be a teacher or a nurse' – and none of us was.

I went straight from school to University in Toronto to do a pure music degree which would also enable me to teach music in high schools. Once I arrived at University, I suddenly realised that there was a whole world beyond music, lots of other very interesting subjects like sociology and philosophy, so I gave it up and took a year off knowing that I never ever wanted to teach music. During this year, I finished a performance associateship course in music at the Royal Conservatorium and then transferred to a small University in the US where I did a course in Fine Arts – art, music, literature and drama. I felt a general Arts education was just what I needed.

Work and life profile

Having graduated with a Fine Arts degree, I went back to Toronto with the main aim of making some money (so that I could travel throughout Europe). After six months of working in a library, I bought my ticket to England and left for London. Having arrived in London, I was pretty horrified once I realised that my saved $1,000 wasn't going to keep me for very long! My parents had helped arrange a 6-month job for me in an insurance company. It paid very little as it was mainly a typing job, and when I left I was a 'temp' for a while.

Then, one day I saw an ad in *Time Out* for a job working for a record company. The actual job description was couched in rather vague terms, so I wrote a cheeky letter more or less saying I wouldn't consider the job unless it meant more responsibility and job satisfaction. It evolved that in fact there were two jobs going, which is why the advertisement had been deliberately vague in its job description. The guy had received hundreds of letter applications but he only chose to interview those people whose letters had stood out – and I was one of them. It turned out that one job required press contacts and the other was for a Radio One 'plugger', which I didn't fancy. I had a picture in my mind of the BBC having a fairly sexist bias which wouldn't work in my favour. I did ask to be kept in mind for any future jobs though.

Shortly afterwards, that company offered me a production assistant type job, which also including some typing (at the time, my sister asked if it meant I had to sleep with the producer!). I stayed for two and a half years and I changed my job role a lot as well as my job title. I became a Production Co-ordinator and looked after record production and the whole process of how records were made. It was a small company so it was easy to see how decisions got made, how contracts were secured and the whole marketing process, etc. I also got involved in learning about copyright laws.

If there were any problems associated with being a woman in the record industry, then I tended not to notice them as any sexist remarks tend to go straight over my head – I just refuse to acknowledge them. Most of the other women were secretaries and I never defined myself in these terms. I do remember one lunchtime meeting when I was asked to go out and get the sandwiches (a job usually done by a secretary). I told them where to go in no uncertain terms and I was never asked again! I think the fact that I was foreign and didn't dress like a dolly bird set me apart. I was also arrogant as I thought my music background made me different, and if I ever came across discrimination I would just put it down to their ignorance.

I then got friendly with a chap who owned his own recording studio and I persuaded him that he needed me to come and work for him. He planned to take me on and teach me about tape copying as well as some multi-track recording techniques. I had become disillusioned with the business considerations of the record business which often superseded considerations of quality resulting in the release, sometimes, of records which the company didn't really believe in. I had the naive fantasy that in the studio business one's sole preoccupation would be with achieving the best possible sound quality. The truth, of course, is that one does the best one can within the time available and within limitations of the budget and artistic priorities of the clients.

My experience as an engineer in the studio gave me an invaluable perception of system analysis and taught me about the whole logic of the mechanics involved in record production. I stayed with them for two years but they ran into financial problems and had to let me and a few other engineers go. After returning from a holiday, the record company I'd previously worked for rang me up and offered me a job as a Marketing Label Manager. The job entailed operating marketing budgets, artist liaisons, etc, dealing with jazz, classical and folk music. A year later the company was taken over and the new people asked me to stay on. But I said no as I was beginning to get dissatisfied and realised that perhaps I just wasn't a record business person.

With the support of an SSRC grant, I got accepted to do an Arts Administration Course at the Central London Polytechnic. It was a one-year full-time course and involved management, marketing and personnel practices, and in particular I hoped it would teach me more about dealing with budgets and finance controls. At the end of the course, we were split into groups and each group had to put on an event. My group helped organise a jazz festival and my role was to be involved in press and promotions. What I learnt most from the course was the concept of how to organise a project from mere assumptions. Since then, it's come up a lot – devising projects and seeing if they are viable.

One of the blokes on the course and I then decided we'd start up our own business as agents for classical and jazz musicians. The business got off the ground and it was very good work experience but our artists were for the most part beginning their career and unless you're very well established it's difficult for young artists to earn enough for you to live off.

During my first year Bill (who is now my husband) financed me as we made virtually no money. (The company still exists by the way.) One day, I rang up Granada Television to ask them to return the tape of one of our clients which I'd sent them. They said, 'Oh, glad you rang, we have a job here that might interest you.'

The job was to be Head of Music, and what was interesting was that at the interview it became clear it involved a mixture of skills I'd already had experience in, e.g. studio work, copyright, organising and developing musical ideas. In fact the only area I hadn't had experience in was negotiating terms with the Musicians' Union. So, I got the job and I enjoy the variety it gives me and keeps me interested – I like to dabble and am a dilettante by nature. With cable and satellite television just around the corner, I need to spend quite a lot of time on copyright, and contracting. I suppose 60–70% of my time is spent on administration and the rest is practical. The fun part of the job is helping producers and directors find the right composers for their programmes. In general, once I've introduced the two, I will then negotiate the contract with the composer or agent, devise and operate the budget, and organise the recording sessions.

I have two men who work in the department but I have no problems and I don't think they find it difficult working with a woman. I think that if you have staff you trust you shouldn't need to tell them what to do all the time. You intervene if they need help or advice and try to be generally supportive. The job carries with it a degree of authority so I don't feel I have to overcome a credibility gap just because I'm a woman. In fact my boss is a woman and is on the Board of Directors.

Handling home/work conflicts

Bill and I have been together a long time and we married recently. Although I'm based in Manchester, I do occasionally have to work in London (as Bill does) and so we have two bases. This means there are many times when we're working and living 250 miles apart and there have been periods when our work locations continually fail to coincide and we almost pass each other on the motorway driving in different directions!

I'm not desperately tidy so I don't need to have a neat household; however, I am getting more fussy about it these days. We've never had any help in the house, mainly because we never get organised enough to find someone to do it. We share the house-duties 50:50 and, if anything, Bill is far more conscientious than I am. He is extremely good and I don't have to explain if I have to work late, for example. And in his own profession as an actor he knows what it's like having unpredictable hours. Bill has always supported me in my work and the relationship just wouldn't have worked if he hadn't.

Given your time over again – would you change anything?

How could I face it all again! Looking back, I think I would have worked a lot harder at school. I was always told from an early age that I was very bright, so I thought I could study without trying and tended to disregard subjects like science. Knowing what I know now, I would have been more aware of the fact that hard work pays off in the long run. If I'd been pushed to be more rigorous intellectually, it may have been more beneficial to me. Everything so far has been by accident rather than design but I suppose I made decisions based on acts of omission. I think I'm aggressive but aggressive in a very laid-back way.

Advice to other women

You have to make other people believe in your capabilities and trust your judgement. Self-confidence without arrogance is therefore a very desirable attribute. If you don't feel very confident, try not to show it. Dressing for the part you have to play is a very good way to give off an air of confidence.

In meetings where there are more men than women you have to find a way of cutting through the discussions if you have something to say and still not appear to be too thrusting. It may well be that you will have to adopt a slightly different approach with some people than you would with others. I am usually quite friendly on meeting people for the first time, but sometimes I get a feeling that the person I meet for the first time is unlikely to take me seriously so I will be rather more steely than normal – after the relationship has been established I can always loosen up but it is often difficult to work it the other way round.

Catherine Robinson – Area Catering Manager, Head of Food Services

Date of birth	5.11.1954
Marital status	Married

Education

–1972	Junior/Middle/Upper School to 'O' level (comprehensive throughout).
1972–1973	College of Further Education for 'Ordinary National Diploma in Business Studies' – gained with Distinction. 'A' Levels in Economics and Sociology.
1973–1976	University and gained BA in Hotel and Management.

Career

1975–1976 (6 months)	Industrial Release 'Swiss Hoteliers Association', spent at hotel in Liestal, Basle, Switzerland.
Sept 1976– Sept 1977	Graduate Management Trainee for large Limited Hotel Company – involved working in many different hotels throughout the UK (residential).
Sept 1977	Junior Assistant Food and Beverage Manager with same hotel company at a tourist spot in the Midlands (residential).
Feb 1978	Promoted to Assistant Food and Beverage Manager at large four star hotel at tourist spot in the north, with same company (residential).
July 1978 (6 weeks)	Period of Relief General Manager at a small hotel with the same company, in a city centre (residential).
Aug 1978	Personnel Manager at a medium-size hotel with same company, at a tourist spot in the Midlands (residential).
Dec 1978– Dec 1979	Food and Beverage/Deputy Hotel Manager at a large Airport Hotel with same company (residential).

Jan 1980	Appointed Unit Catering Manager in large industrial firm.
Sept 1980	Assistant Area Catering Manager with same firm.
Oct 1983– Present	Area Catering Manager, Head of Food Services for twelve Units (6,000 meals daily, in charge of 140 personnel). (Same firm.)

Family background

I am second of four daughters. My father is a headmaster and my mother a lecturer, so I was brought up with every opportunity to take advantage of the educational system. Indeed, both my parents always encouraged me to make the most of myself and my future. For instance, at one time I was interested in nursing and my parents obtained details of degrees in nursing which would lead to a more 'rewarding' type of career.

As it happened though, 'Hotel and Catering' became my chosen career path. As a teenager, I spent a week at a park centre which involved working as a General Assistant on a cafeteria counter. I really enjoyed the job and loved the social interactions and the variety of work involved. I also felt that if I went to University, I wanted to train for something that had a purpose so to speak, and that would increase my chances of getting a job at the end!

Although my final career choice was catering (and I ended up doing a BA in Hotel and Management), in my view I think the advice given to teenage girls when it comes to career guidance is still very poor. In retrospect, I may have chosen a less 'female-type' career if I'd had more knowledge, for example, of what an engineer did. (The reason I mention engineering is that recently at work I was introduced to a female graduate trainee in engineering – and she was the first one I'd ever met!)

I should add, however, that during my time at University I was never made to feel in any way unequal. In fact at least half the people on my course were female.

Work and life profile

I found my first job as a management trainee to be most interesting, with lots of variety. Unfortunately, in the first few months I was very troubled by a male middle-aged Personnel Manager, who picked on me as not only was I female but I think he was also jealous of the fact that I had a degree and he didn't. He'd make up stories about me that just weren't true and report them to the Training Manager – stupid things such as my hair being untidy! Being young and inexperienced, this 'gentleman' (due to his resentment of women) reduced me to tears. Luckily, I was fortunate enough to have an understanding female Training Manager (who I think had had similar problems with him before), and she helped me through it and to come out 'on top'.

Being under 25, female, and in charge as a Deputy Manager of many different hotels was both hard-work and fun. Undoubtedly, being a woman, the challenge was much greater than it would have been for any male. The expression on some people's faces when I turned up at their request to see the manager was often quite comical! Occasionally, people inferred that as a woman I couldn't possibly do the job of an hotel manager as well as a man, as it involved having to be physically strong. My reply would always be that if the men were doing their jobs properly, then as managers they should not be physically lifting barrels of beer from the cellar but do as I did and get the labourer(s) to do the work. I also pointed out that I was quite capable of changing a beer barrel, although like many men I was unable to lift a full one containing 22 gallons.

You do learn by your mistakes and I learnt pretty quickly that you didn't make yourself vulnerable for sexual advances by men by going unaccompanied into guests' bedrooms to check an 'out-of-order' television or to investigate a complaint!

During my final job in hotels I was 25 years old and Deputy Hotel Manager, with an Area Manager in his late 50s who thought of women as sex objects (and coincidentally was recently separated from his wife). Consequently, my successes in the Food and Beverage Sector really didn't count for much when it came to be considered for promotion. The final crunch came when a hopeless male Personnel Manager (below me in status and younger) was offered a General Manager's job. He refused it for domestic reasons, and even then they didn't consider me for the job – I just don't think it crossed their minds. I realised that I was in a 'Catch 22' situation and I *had* to get out and move to another company or I'd remain well and truly stuck. (Men are not faced with such dilemmas and, to be honest, even when women are, nine times out of 10, they fail to acknowledge the true situation. There's this tendency to believe they are not as good as the men – which in my mind is a misconception and merely an excuse for not taking risks and moving on elsewhere.)

And so I applied for two jobs and got interviews for both. I decided to get away from the residential side that so many hotels insist upon for their managers, and go into Industrial Catering instead. I was offered the first job I went for, so I cancelled the second job interview. Within six months of my new appointment I was promoted and took the position on three months later. Twelve months later I had a period of deputising for my boss, then in October 1983 I was appointed Area Catering Manager.

My present job involves supervising and controlling 12 different Catering Units. The work involves a lot of travelling and no day is ever the same. I have direct input to policy decisions and I feel most comfortable in this job, having encountered no serious difficulties related to the fact that I am a woman. In fact I was the first female to attend a monthly meeting, and since my appointment two other women have been taken on from outside the firm, at a similar status to mine.

Handling home/work conflicts

I think that it's social attitudes, as well as those held by people I work with, which are the hardest to ignore. These can exert considerable pressure upon you as an individual. For example, many people still like to think you hold the traditional belief that 'a woman's place is in the home'! The way I handle comments such as: 'How does your husband cope when you are away on a course?' is by answering, 'Very well, he's been well trained!' I find the best thing is to invite humour without creating conflict.

Another common potential conflict comment involves the reference to the rights and wrongs of being a working wife or mother. The best way I've found for dealing with this is to stress that what is right for you is not necessarily right for another individual and that every case is different. This type of approach doesn't put you in conflict with someone like the Managing Director, for example, whose wife probably gave up work when she had her first baby!

Having been married for one year, I can honestly say that I have no home/work conflicts. The household jobs are shared with my husband and we support each other in every way. Actually, any home conflicts are created by *other people* who may think, for example, that I should do all the ironing – which is out of the question, as it is shared.

Given your time over again – would you change anything?
No.

Advice to other women

Don't squash your own capabilities because those above you don't think you are worth developing and assume that you are not interested in career progression, merely because you are a woman. They are labelling you in accordance with their own beliefs. What is important is what you *believe* and *want*.

Always let your employer know if you are interested in promotion. If you don't get it, then move firms. Sometimes just applying for other jobs lets everyone realise you are serious and not just the 'token woman'. You must do whatever you feel is right for you, and don't let people you work with, or family or friends, influence your decisions as far as the type of job you do, your domestic duties, whether you should take maternity leave, and so on.

Postscript

I have often referred to myself as being 'career minded', and I believe it is important that my boss knows this fact, as women often stop being 'career centred' and become what is traditionally called 'family centred'. I am particularly vulnerable to getting this label at this stage of my career, owing to the fact that I recently got married. I'm therefore determined not to allow it to happen.

Finally, while I look forward to weekends when I can relax with my husband, I also look forward to going to work – the balance for me is exactly right!

Ruth Smith – Film Producer – Head of Production

Date of birth	10 August 1953
Education	Kindergarten/Prep School/Grammar School to 'O' Level
May/June 1971	Sixth Form College 'A' Levels
July 1971/Aug 1972	Travelled abroad.
Sept 1972/June 1974	Studied at College of Further Education for Diploma of Business Studies, Economics and Marketing.
Career	
July 1974/Jan 1980	Worked for advertising agency as writer/producer rising to position of Creative Director/Producer.
March 1980	Joined Film Production Company as Producer.
Jan 1981	Left work to have baby.
May 1981	Gave birth to baby boy.
March 1982	Returned to work full-time – having in the interim done some freelance work at home.
Jan 1983	Joined present company of Film Producers.
Feb 1984	Appointed Head of Production with Film Production Company.

Family background

My father owns a business so I grew up in a 'business' family. I'm the only girl. My five brothers regularly helped in the business during school holidays and there was never any suggestion that I couldn't also be involved. In fact, all the men who featured strongly in my childhood – i.e. uncles, family friends and the like – were their own bosses!

The idea of running a business or being my own boss was therefore a very natural aspiration. I was never treated any differently by my father, in a working context, because I was female but I do know that my mother felt there was something 'slightly unfeminine' about a young woman who 'too actively' pursued a business career. Mummy had many friends in professional theatre – that was all right – but business was to her a masculine pursuit.

I attended an 'all girls' private school as a day pupil and I now think that had I been sent to a mixed school I would have been better able to deal with boys/men of my own age in my late teens and early twenties. I wouldn't have been so easily embarrassed by teasing for example – I would have understood the game. I didn't experience this problem when I first started work because I was dealing with men on terms that I'd been familiar with from early childhood, business terms! Perhaps that's why, at an age when many of my friends and contemporaries were working hard at building up a social circle I was working hard at building a career (without really knowing I was doing it)! After gaining 'A' levels in English, Use of English and History, I had no clear idea of what I wanted to do so I went abroad for a year. While abroad I applied to do an Arts degree but when I returned home to take up my studies I changed my mind at the last moment. I suddenly realised that I'd probably end up teaching and that was one thing I knew I didn't want to do. Instead, I chose a two-year diploma course in Business Studies, Economics and Marketing. This course included shorthand and typewriting, both of which have proved extremely useful skills.

Work and life profile

The only things I was ever really sure I enjoyed were writing and language, so my first job was with an advertising agency as a junior copywriter. I stayed with the company for five years and was promoted during that time, first to senior copywriter, shortly afterwards to the Board of Directors and finally to Creative Director. Within months of joining the agency I became involved in the production of television work, so I was learning the craft of production almost from the word go. I knew immediately that it was this area of the industry on which I wanted to concentrate and so I worked hard and learned quickly.

I recognised my luck in being in the right place at the right time; the agency gave me the opportunity early in my career to work with very good producers and directors from whom I could learn. I had the further good fortune to be working for three men who willingly taught me the practical side of running a business and 'managing' people. I respected all three men and got on well with them. What I lacked in experience I made up for in enthusiasm and I wasn't alone in that. Two young men who joined the company at the same time were similarly encouraged and rewarded. I was the only woman working in that capacity at first but other women joined the company over the period and I was replaced by a woman. My place on the Board, however, went to a male colleague when I left. This wasn't bias, it was simply that at that time he was the best qualified for the position.

I decided to give up the security of the agency and go freelance as a producer. Again the agency was helpful in initially supplying me with work which helped me establish myself. My husband was also extremely supportive. The fact that he too works in the film industry counts for a lot because he understands what I'm doing and is often able to help. Shortly after going freelance I was offered a job as a producer with a film production company. I stayed with the company for one year. When I left to have a baby they made it clear that I could come back at any time if I wanted to. When I did decide to return to work I didn't approach the company because in the interim people had changed and I felt it might be foolish to go over old ground with new faces.

Originally I intended to give up full-time work and concentrate on being a mother. After the baby was born I did some freelance work from home. It seemed important at the time to preserve some independence in terms of cash flow and to 'keep my hand in'. I found that although I had work to do I tended to concentrate my energies on the baby at first. I'm sure I did try to play the perfect wife and mother role as well as doing my freelance work, but after a while I realised that it wasn't very practical.

When our son was about eight months old I discussed with my husband the idea of a part-time job away from the house. I missed people contact and the busy atmosphere of work. It was years since I'd attended any job interviews so I decided to apply for some jobs just for interview experience. Within a couple of days of our conversation my husband arrived home with a copy of an advertisement for a writer/producer with an advertising agency. I applied and was genuinely surprised when they offered me the job almost on the spot. Through an excellent employment agency I quickly found a superb nanny and so, almost by accident, I returned to full-time employment when my son was 10 months old. Unfortunately the job didn't turn out to be what I'd expected. I couldn't do my job as I'd been trained to do it and I found the constant lectures from the Vice-Chairman exhausting. He was constantly telling me how FEMININE his wife was and how he (and she?) believed that a woman's place is in the home '. . . especially when children are small! . . .' After 10 months of trying to get things to change even a little I gave up and decided to leave. The only good thing about beating your head against a brick wall is the relief when you stop. This experience did cause me to question myself seriously. I wondered whether being at home for a while with a baby had changed me. Whether I was wrong and couldn't see it.

The production company I'm now with offered me a job as soon as they heard I was on the move from the agency. I've come full circle really. Like my first company, this one is owned by three very professional, experienced and capable men. I do my job as well as I possibly can and I'm invited more and more to participate in the overall running of the company. I'm not planning to move for a long time. I completed my first year with the company by being promoted to Head of Production and it was suggested that good results over the next year/18 months could lead to a partnership.

My job as a producer involves me in the planning and

making of all sorts of films. I work in conjunction with a director to decide how best to shoot any given job and how long it will take to shoot and edit. Having worked these factors out I assess the costs. It's normal for a client to approach two or three producers before deciding who will actually do the work and his decision will be influenced by my costs, my choice of director and our interpretation of the brief. There is a certain amount of personality involved in the whole transaction. You might get everything right but simply not hit it off with the person you are dealing with. Equally, you might get on well but another producer might suggest something which makes the client feel more confident about going elsewhere. Obviously there is choice on both sides. Once I've got the job it's up to me to make sure that it's finished to brief on time and on budget. There are aspects of my job which might be made easier if I was a man. I suppose it might be more difficult for some male clients to deal with me if they're not used to doing business with women. When working in London, for example, some clients might expect a male producer to take them 'on the town'. Doing the clubs, etc, is obviously easier, if equally tedious, for a male producer. I think if I tried to compete in this area I'd just make clients uncomfortable. When I take clients to lunch I naturally make the booking in my name. Although I ask the waiter for the wine list, which helps him identify who's doing the entertaining, I usually ask the client if he would like to choose the wine. Not all men like a woman taking charge in a semi-social situation and my goal is to put my guest at his ease.

My aim is to be the best producer I can be. I am a woman working in a male-dominated environment but I'm not aware that my being female creates any particular problem. I don't expect any advantages because I'm female nor do I expect any disadvantages! I like being female and I like being feminine but when I'm working surely the fact that my body is a different shape is irrelevant . . . my brain is just as good.

I certainly wouldn't resent other female producers coming to work for the company and capable, ambitious secretaries would be encouraged by me to seek advancement. I find myself dealing with women more frequently, both as clients and suppliers, as time passes. I must admit I do like working with men. Many of my friends are men and I'm used to working with men – maybe it has something to do with having five brothers.

Handling home/work conflicts

To strike a balance, be good at my job and be a successful wife and mother can be difficult. For the first few months back at work I fully expected to walk in one evening and hear my son say 'Go away you don't care for me.' I now realise that it's quality of time and not quantity that counts with children. When I get home I try to be consistent. We talk, play, read stories, sing songs all very much to an established pattern. Sometimes all I want to do is put my feet up and have a drink but that will just have to wait until my son is a little older. On the advice of my brother, who is a child psychiatrist, we have a 'private time' each day. Evening has proved better than morning, and our private time consists of spending about an hour together in his room before my son goes to bed. No-one else is allowed to join in at this time – it is strictly a time when he and I can work at our relationship. He calls his bedroom his 'safe place' so this is where the hour is normally spent.

As I said before I have a very good nanny. I do think, though, that it's very difficult to assess what a nanny is going to be like in an interview. I talked to mine for about an hour. Then she spent some time with the baby while I watched from the side lines and after a while I joined in to see how he would react to both of us together. Initially I left them together while I went out to do shopping, etc and we built up the length of time I was away gradually as he got to know her. One should choose a nanny who will fit personality-wise with the parents as well as with the child. Look for a similar sense of humour, for example. If you smoke don't appoint someone who hates cigarettes, use common sense. The biggest problem is choosing someone who is consistent and will stay with you for a few years. I've known people who've had nannies who got bored after six months and moved on. Check references carefully. Note how frequently she has changed jobs in the past. Make sure she has actually worked with children of the ages of your family before.

171

I think my time at home looking after a baby and sticking to a routine helped me be more organised when I returned to work. I try to do the shopping on a Thursday night so that on Saturdays we can enjoy a leisurely breakfast. I clean the house on Saturday mornings and then relax in the afternoon with my family. We used to have a cleaning lady but we found it easier to do the cleaning ourselves. My husband sees to at least 50% of the housework and taking care of our son. I'm sure it's vital to have this sort of support from your partner. Most of all it helps if he knows what your job involves and understands the pressures.

Given your time over again – would you change anything?

In the back of my mind I was always attracted to writing and film work but I wasn't sure how to go about 'getting in'. Given my time over again I wouldn't change anything.

Advice to other women

When you start work, find good teachers and watch and listen to them. Forget that you're female, don't expect favours because you're female, and don't expect to get away with things. Be determined, work hard and pay attention to how you sound and look – in other words behave like any normal young executive. Before accepting a job assess if possible the attitudes of the people you'll be working for. Look at what women already with the company have achieved. How far have they progressed and over what period of time? It is hard to break away from secretarial work but it's not impossible. Secretaries who do get promoted in the same company often find that they're never allowed to forget they were secretaries. As soon as someone takes a holiday or leaves they're asked to fill in and it can be very frustrating. For that reason promotion out of secretarial work is often better sought through a move to a new company. If you don't do things for yourself, other people won't do them for you. Try to look and sound confident even when you're not. My stomach still turns over sometimes when I have to talk with or meet new people, but I say to myself 'other people can do it so I can too!'

Postscript

I've never referred to myself as a 'career woman'; it is just a label. I enjoy my home and my family but I also need the stimulation of work to feel that I'm getting as much out of my life as I can.

Elizabeth MacDonald-Brown – Marketing Director

Date of Birth	16.2.38
Marital Status	Married
Education	London University extra-mural Diploma in Sociology.
	Miscellaneous courses on Market Research, Marketing, New Product Development, General Management at business school in Switzerland, Effective Speaking and Broadcasting.
Lecturing	Lecturer at (and Convenor of) various Market Research Society and ESOMAR Courses on New Product Development, Marketing Research and Test Marketing and at miscellaneous seminars on Marketing and Social Responsibility, Advertising Control Systems, the Office of Fair Trading and Consumer Affairs.

Career

1955–1958	Murex Limited Analytical Assistant.
1958–1960	Colgate Palmolive Limited Market Research Assistant, Research Executive.
1961–1962	Data Collection Limited Market Research Executive.
1962–1970 (1962–1966)	The Nestlé Company Limited Senior Research Executive.
(1966–1970)	Manager – Head of Marketing Research department ($£\frac{1}{3}$ million budget) comprising 70 permanent/250 part-time staff, executing all research for the Nestlé Group, including Crosse & Blackwell, Findus and Maggi. Responsible (with 2 others) for the Nestlé Group's Diversification and Acquisition policy. Held key role in Group's marketing planning.

173

Career continued

1970–1973	Yardley International Limited Marketing Services Manager and subsequently Main Board Director – Advising Managing Director/Regional Management for Europe, Far East, Africa and South America on corporate policies and marketing strategies. Planning and controlling the Company's new product and packaging development and all centrally generated advertising and promotional material.
1974	Married Jonathan Brown (now Staff-Director Business & Financial Planning, Austin-Rover).
1974–1978	Office of Fair Trading Consumer Affairs Division. Preparing proposals for changing the laws relating to advertising and promotion; price claims; packaging and labelling. Responsible for OFT liaison with the Advertising Industry, in particular the Advertising Standards Authority.
August 1978	Twins born.
August 1978– May 1984	Caring for children, plus small amount of marketing consultancy.
October 1981 – end 1983	Non-Executive Director of major food company. Member of Consultative board assisting in determining a long-term plan for UB (Biscuits), mainly in response to a major McKinsey Report.
June 1st 1984 – current	Knight Frank & Rutley Marketing Director.

Additional business activities

1982 – current	Member of Institute of Marketing's Business Development and Employment Committee.
1982 – current	British Footwear Marketing Awards – a judge.
1983 – current	Institute of Marketing's National Marketing Awards – an adjudicator.

174

Family background

My father was a bricklayer with well-developed practical skills; but he had unconventional ways of thinking, which made him an unusual and unconventional man. He would always question things and never simply accept things on face value. Consequently, as a child I was always encouraged to find out facts for myself; I remember I always had a thirst for knowledge. I was the second born and had three brothers. On most matters, I don't think my parents treated me particularly differently because I was the only girl, but I do remember my mother stressing marriage – something I don't believe she did with my brothers.

At 16 years of age, due to family financial considerations and the fact that my mother thought I'd end up getting married and hence not need a career, it was necessary for me to leave school and get a paid job.

Work and life profile

My first job was as a laboratory assistant in a chemical company, but working with the chemicals affected me. I also decided at this time to continue my education and enrolled for a London University extra-mural course (at evening classes), studying social history and social structure for two years. At the age of 18, I moved away from home to central London and whilst continuing with the London University course (now social psychology) one of the other students mentioned job openings at Colgate Palmolive. I was accepted by Colgate as a market research interviewer and was rapidly promoted every nine months. At the age of 20 I was a Field Manager, responsible for four teams of permanent interviewers, and several months later I was offered the position of Research Executive. I remember during my time with Colgate Palmolive one worked incredibly long hours and we were often there at 11 o'clock at night. I believe people succeed due to striving, drive and a willingness to recognise and accept good help when offered. Personally, I thrive on pressure, it brings out the best in me; isolated in an ivory tower I would not produce a work of art. I remember throughout this period I kept thinking, 'I really will leave and go and live and work in Paris, *but* I'll just do this next job first, it will make my CV look better when I return.'

Then I decided to move to Data Collection Ltd, an independent research agency, where I worked on everything from underwear to steel tubes. However, this company was going bankrupt, so I then moved, after some difficulty, to Nestlé as the Group Head in charge of (instant) coffee research. All four colleagues at the same level were men, but after four years I was made a (Research) manager and became Nestlé's first female manager world-wide. Being the first in the (Nestlé) world, the appointment was considered somewhat novel and everyone (on training programmes) used to come and have a look at me. At the age of 27, I was now in charge of research budgets totalling some millions of pounds – at current prices. I always tended to increase my age as I looked rather young. Consequently, reaching 30 (or indeed 40) was no adjustment for me!

I was with the Nestlé company for eight years. Then, at the age of 31, one of the Directors who had left to join Yardley International asked me if I'd like to work for Yardley. I joined as a Marketing Services Manager and subsequently was made a Main Board Director. In this job, being female had little, if any, impact, as cosmetic companies (including Yardley) have a long tradition of employing female managers – a level of impartiality exists which is still rare in the business world. At this time I wasn't married and, indeed, hadn't met anyone whom I wished to marry (or vice-versa). I looked on marriage as a tremendous commitment and I was terrified of it. I also think, perhaps wrongly, that being married would have been disadvantageous to my career to that date. I know I was unsuitable marriage material during my twenties; although my business acumen was reasonably advanced, emotionally I was somewhat green. All my drives and energies went mainly into my work.

In 1974 (aged 35) I married and freely admit that I had no concept as to what marriage really meant until I actually became 'a wife'. My husband (Jonathan Brown) had done an MBA at Harvard and was just tackling a new job. I didn't wish to continue the travelling away from home required by my job and so decided to take a more regular job, in terms of hours. (I'd observed in other marriages how when both partners are working full pelt at a similar level, often the marriage doesn't work.) So, I applied for a position in the Office of Fair Trading (OFT) in their Consumer Affairs Division and accepted a contract appointment. At that time, John Methven was Director General of the OFT.

Then, in 1978, our twins were born and I continued to work part-time professionally in both paid and unpaid capacities. My part-time business activities have included marketing consultancy and being a Non-Executive Director of a major food company, plus work on the Institute of Marketing's Business Development and Employment Committee. During a career gap, it's very important not to lose touch with the business world and to keep up-to-date. My children are now at full-time day school and, consequently, I am now looking for the right full-time paid job.

Handling home/work conflicts

If one marries, then it's crucial to marry someone who enjoys the fact that his wife works and is prepared to accept all the aspects – the benefits of having a stimulating partner, intellectually, as well as the extra pressures caused by two careers in one household. Anyone who has resistance towards their wife working will get more resistant as time goes by. I must say that, at first, I had to go through a type of trade-union negotiation with my husband about sharing household duties. The division of labour in our household is reasonably fair – but not necessarily conventional!

My business training has been of tremendous benefit to me, and when tackling any functional aspects at home I look at it as a business task with the main aim being to reduce effort. I think that being efficient and organised at home should give me time to enjoy my leisure activities (it doesn't always work!). I buy three months' supply of 'our fast moving domestic lines' at a time, but cooking food for the freezer has *never* become a hobby of mine – M & S do it rather better. I feel women should invest (where finances permit) in reliable machinery to help them in running a home and, if they can afford it, employ domestic or childcare help. We did have various mother's helps when the children were young, but we found it difficult to find long-term, reliable helpers. We gave up outside help for a whole year due to disasters with childcare help. However, we now have a general helper (Christine) who also collects the children from school. It's wonderful having such good and flexible help and it makes a tremendous difference; I hope she is as happy with us as we are with her. Finally, I think it's very important to get one's priorities right and it is essential to plan for leisure time with one's partner – even if it means holding off doing domestic chores.

Given your time over again – would you change anything?

I don't think it's possible for me to say I would do anything differently in my work or personal life, as due to my character and personality the *pattern* of things would probably be the same. I would have liked to have gone to University; but I may eventually do an Open University degree as an old age pensioner! I've always been a permanent evening-school student and even took up the social sciences course again (studying social philosophy) after a gap of ten years.

If I ever found myself in a job where I was being put down, then I'd leave. As a woman, I would never allow myself to be exploited, or paid less than the market rate for the job. In earlier days, I felt I was representing women who would follow me. On promotion, I was once offered a lower salary than my male predecessor, so I asked the Managing Director a simple question, i.e. 'This is *not* logical – please would you explain it to me?' My salary was soon increased. I believe everything can be turned into a learning experience. I think the reason for my own success, if any, is that I have a mind suitable for today's business climate; I'm a good, detached analyst and I have drive and determination. I'm also (amazingly enough) a good listener and I watch people carefully when I interact with them. Even if I was working somewhere as an apple grader, I'd be concerned about the company's profits and feel I was responsible for the bottom line. I get a real high and thrill from solving business problems. I look back on my work experiences as being phenomenally interesting, whilst not always happy – I don't think you can ask for more than that.

Advice to other women

You should get the best possible career qualifications you can afford – preferably, a full-time, professional business school education. Just never give up – if someone strives to succeed, despite everything, they will.

As regards the home/work issue – you must be organised, buy time-saving equipment, fix priorities with your partner and make sure you leave time for leisure activities. My husband says I'm very efficient and we enjoy our leisure together and with our children. For example, we try to take the children to (their) parties together and chat in the car. Often, when we arrive, we're the only 'couple' who have jointly brought their children; of course, others may consider this a mis-use of time.

Finally, I believe anyone in a management job *and* wishing to continue their career is unwise to give it up to have children (my circumstances were a little exceptional, being 40 and having twins). Having a career gap definitely affects one's future career – if your career is a top priority to you, it is crucial to prepare and to set up childcare arrangements in order to return to work after maternity leave. I think one should plan for a return to work after pregnancy carefully and there is a need for more education, counselling and pamphlets, etc in business organisations about this issue. Above all there is a need for more flexible patterns of employment for males and females.

In the final analysis, I suppose I have always taken risks in my career. I've left highly comfortable jobs and I've never thought about my pension! However, I remembered to tether my camel!

Postscript

To end where I began, as from June 1st 1984, I have a new job as Knight Frank & Rutley's Marketing Director. At last, I'm selling all the services connected with land, bricks and mortar; perhaps my father might think I have a 'proper job' at last!

SUMMARY

If you read the accounts of the working and personal lives of these five women it becomes evident that they share many characteristics:

- They all refused to acknowledge the possibility that being female could prove disadvantageous as far as career success was concerned.

- They refused to accept any sort of discrimination.

- They chose partners carefully and tended to transfer business skills into their domestic lives.

- They were all prepared to take risks and leave jobs that offered limited prospects (even comfortable jobs).

- And finally – they were all *confident about their abilities and determined to succeed and REACH FOR THE TOP!*

Useful Addresses

Careers, Training and Advisory Bodies

Business Education Council, 168–173 High Holborn, London WC1

Careers and Occupational Information Centre (COIC), MSC, Moorfoot, Sheffield S1 4Q

Careers Research Advisory Centre (CRAC), Bateman Street, Cambridge

Central Services Unit (CSU), Crawford House, Precinct Centre, Oxford Road, Manchester M13 9EP

Centre for Research on European Women (CREW), 22 Rue de Toulouse, 1040 Brussels, Belgium

Cosmopolitan Courses, National Magazine House, 72 Broadwick Street, London W1V 2BP

Department of Employment, OB2 Caxton House, Tothill Street, London SW1H 9HA

Department of Trade and Industry, Victoria Street, London SW1

Directory of EGA Services for Adults, Educational Advisory Services Project, The Open University, Fairfax House, Mervion Street, Leeds LS2 8JU

The Equal Opportunities Commission, Overseas House, Quay Street, Manchester M3 3AN

Equal Pay and Opportunity Campaign, 59 Canonbury Park North, London N1

European Foundation for Management Development, 20 Place Stephanie, B-1050, Brussels, Belgium

The Industrial Society, Robert Hyde House, 48 Bryanston Square, London W1H 7LN

Manpower Services Commission Training Division, MSC, Moorfoot, Sheffield S1 4Q

National Advisory Centre on Careers for Women, Drayton House, 30 Gordon Street, London WC1H 0AY

National Association of Educational Guidance Services (NAEGS), 66 Newlands Avenue, Melton Park, Newcastle-Upon-Tyne NE3 5PY

National Organisation for Women's Management Education (NOWME), 29 Burkes Road, Beaconsfield, Bucks

Options Career Workshops, Sarah Weston, Options, 19 Belmont Road, Twickenham, Middlesex TW2 5DA

Professional and Executive Recruitment (PER), 4–5 Grosvenor Place, London SW1X 7SB

Rights for Women Unit, National Council for Civil Liberties, 186 Kings Cross Road, London WC1X 9DE

Rights of Women in Europe Group (ROW), 10 Tredegar Road, London E3

TUC Women's Advisory Committee, Congress House, Great Russell Street, London WC1

Women and Training News, Ann Cooke, Group Co-ordinator, c/o Department of Management Studies, Gloucestershire College of Arts and Technology, Oxshills Lane, Gloucester GL2 9HW

The Women at Work Unit, UMIST, PO Box 88, Manchester M60 1QD

Network Groups

The 300 Group, The Mill House, Burford, Oxon

The Academic Women's Achievement Group, Susan Hutchinson, Hon. Secretary, Computer Centre, University College, Gower Street, London WC1W 6BT

Association of Personal Assistants and Secretaries, 14 Victoria Terrace, Royal Leamington Spa, Warwickshire

Association of Women in Enterprise, The Old Stable, Upper Station Road, Henfield, West Sussex

Association of Women in Public Relations, Judith Turner, Vice President and Hon. Membership Secretary, 193 Chiltern Court, Baker Street, London NW1

The Association of Women Solicitors, Law Society's Hall, 113 Chancery Lane, London WC2

British Association of Women Executives, 303 Preston Road, Harrow, Middlesex MA3 0QQ

British Women Pilots' Association, 25 Foubert's Place, London W1V 2AL

The Executive Secretaries Association, 45 Milford Close, Abbey Wood, London SE2 0DS

The Fawcett Society, Parnell House, 5th Floor, 25 Wilton Road, London SW1V 1LW

Focus, 158–160 Sutherland Avenue, London W9

Girls and Mathematics Association, c/o Girls and Mathematics Project, University of London Institute of Education, 58 Gordon Square, London WC1

Institute of Qualified Private Secretaries, 126 Farnham Road, Slough SL1 4XA

International Toastmistress Clubs, Susan Plumtree – Publicity Officer, c/o Help the Aged, 146 Queen Victoria Street, London EC4

National Association of Women Pharmacists, Christine Glover, 36 Garvock Hill, Dunfermline, Fife

Network, 8 Thornton Place, London W1H 1FG

United Kingdom, Federation of Business and Professional Women, 23 Ansdell Street, Kensington, London W8 5BN

Women and Computing, c/o A Woman's Place, 48 William IV Street, London WC1

Women's Film, Television and Video Network, 79 Wardour Street, London W1V 3PH

Women in Banking, Ann Watts, National Westminster Bank, Planning and Projects Dept., International Banking Division, 36th floor, National Westminster Tower, 25 Broad Street, London EC2

Women in the Civil Service, Rita O'Brien, Room 373, Department of Industry, Ashdown House, 123 Victoria Street, London SW1

Women in Industry, 11 Redpit, Dilton Marsh, Westbury, Wilts

Women in Libraries, 8 Hill Road, London NW8

Women in Management, 4 Mapledale Avenue, Croydon CR0 5TA

Women in Medicine, 10 Sotherby Road, London N5 2UR

Women in Personnel Management, Margaret Warren, c/o Consumer's Association, 15 Buckingham Street, London WC2

Women in Printing Trades Group, c/o Community Press, 2A St Paul's Road, London N1

Women in Publishing, Information Officer, 48 Kings Road, Long Ditton, Surrey KT 6 5JH

Women in Telecom, c/o Denise McGuire, IN3-2-31, Room 116, Lintas House, 15–19 New Fetter Lane, London EC4

The Women's Advertising Club of London, Mrs J. Lovell, Hon. Secretary, IFF Research Ltd, 12 Argyll Street, London W1V 1AB

The Women's Engineering Society, 25 Foubert's Place, London W1V 2AL

The Women's Travel Club of Great Britain, 38 Avarn Road, London SW17

Zonta International, Ileana Macmillan, 22 Springfield Meadows, Weybridge, Surrey KT 13 8AJ

Suggested Reading

High Pressure: Working Lives of Women Managers by C.L. Cooper and M. Davidson, Fontana Paperbacks (1982)

Stress and the Woman Manager by M.J. Davidson and C. Cooper, Martin Robertson (1983)

Working Women: An International Survey by M. Davidson and C. Cooper (Editors), Wiley (1984)

Women in Management by C. Cooper and M. Davidson (Editors), Heinemann (1984)

The New Executive Woman by M.G. Williams, A Mentor Book, New English Library Ltd. (1977)

Women in Management by B.A. Stead, Prentice-Hall (1978)

The Managerial Woman by M. Hennig and A. Jardim, Pan (1979)

Women Managers: Travellers in A Male World by Judi Marshall, John Wiley and Sons (1984)

Sexual Harassment at Work by S. Read, Hamlyn Paperbacks (1982)

Positive Action for Women – the Next Step by S. Robarts with A. Coote and E. Ball, NCCL (1981)

Cosmopolitan's Guide to Getting Ahead by Jones, Ebury Press (1982)

Work Challenge by Garnett, The Industrial Society (1983)

The Stress Check by C.L. Cooper, Prentice-Hall (1981)

Subject Women by A. Oakley, Oxford (1981)

Superwoman by S. Conran, Penguin (1977)

Man Made Language by D. Spender, Routledge and Kegan Paul (1980)

Women at Work by J. Glew, Pitman (1979)

Women's Rights in the Workplace by T. Gilland and L. Whitty, Penguin (1983)

Cosmopolitan's Careers Guide by C. Faulder, The National Magazine Company (1979)

Equal Opportunities: A Career Guide by R. Miller, Penguin (1981)

Danger: Men at Work by R. Miles, MacDonald Futura (1983)

Back to Work: A Practical Guide for Women by C. Moulder and P. Sheldon, Kogan Page (1979)

185

Reach for the Top

How to Survive as a Working Mother by L. Garner, Penguin (1980)
Women × Two – How to Cope with a Double Life by M. Kenny, Hamlyn Paperbacks (1979)
Your Perfect Right: A Guide to Assertive Behaviour by R.E. Alberti and M.L. Evans, Impact (1970)
When I Say No, I Feel Guilty by M.J. Smith, New York: Bantam Books (1975)
The Assertive Woman by S. Phelps and N. Austin, Impact (1975)
Self Assertion for Women by P. Butler, Harper and Row (1976)
A Woman in Your Own Right by A. Dickson, Quartet Books (1982)
The Small Business Guide by C. Barrow, BBC Publications (1982)
Small Business Kit by D.S. Watkins *et al*, National Extension College (1982)
Careers Guide published annually by COIC, 166 High Holborn, London WC1V 6P
CNAA Compendium of Degree Courses, free from the Council for National Academic Awards, 344–354 Gray's Inn Road, London WC1X 8BP
Degree Course Guides, a series of 40 booklets published by CRAC/Hobson Press, Bateman Street, Cambridge
Compendium of Advanced Courses in Colleges of Further and Higher Education, DES Advisory Council, Tavistock House South, Tavistock Square, London WC1
Polytechnic Courses Handbook, Committee of Directors of Polytechnics, 309 Regent Street, London W1

Free MSC Publications from Ginny Ellis, Assistant to Group Co-ordinator, The Co-ordinating Group for the Development of Training for Women, c/o Department of Management Studies, Gloucestershire College of Arts & Technology, Oxshills Lane, Gloucester GL2 9HW, include:
No Barriers Here?
Practical Approaches to Women's Career Development
Women and Training News
Managing or Removing the Career Break
A Re-entry and Retrainer Scheme for Women
Women Managers: Their Problems and What can be done To Help Them
Equalising Opportunities for Women in the Printing and Publishing Industries
Career/Life Planning Workshops for Women Managers: Give us a Break
Employee Potential: Issues in the Development of Women
The Right Woman for the Job
Secretarial Work in Central London 1970–1981
Personal Effectiveness for Women
Women, Work and Training
Case Studies in the Simmons Method

Numerous free publications are also available from the Equal Opportunities Commission, Overseas House, Quay Street, Manchester M3 3HW and include:
Positive Action – Have You Tried it Yet?
Day Release for Girls

Fresh Start (where women can train for a new job)
Positive Sex Discrimination in Training Schemes
Job Sharing
Equal Pay for Women
A Short Guide to the Sex Discrimination Act
How to Prepare Your Own Case for an Industrial Tribunal
I Want to work ... but What About the Kids?
*Alternative Models of group child-care for Pre-school Children with Working
    Parents*
Day Care for School Age Children
Nurseries in Colleges and Universities
*Social Networks and Job Information: the Situation of Women Who Return to
    Work*
Parity Begins at Home
Parenthood in the Balance
New Technology and Women's Employment
The Fact About Women Is ...
What is the EOC and how can it help me?
A Brief Guide to the EOC Information Centre

Index